Help!

You're Self

The only non self help book
you'll never need

John Glyn Hughes

Copyright © 2017 John Glyn Hughes

All rights reserved.

ISBN-10: 154294502X
ISBN-13: 978-1542945028

DEDICATION

To Mandy, Catherine and Bethan for putting up with the tap, tapping…but it wasn't going to write itself!

And for those who think, feel, care & share.

CONTENTS

Introduction

Chapter 1. Life

Chapter 2. Happiness

Chapter 3. People

Chapter 4. Contemplations

ACKNOWLEDGMENTS

This book was born from what initially was meant to be a series of short articles that I had intended to share with a small collective group on the blog of my website. One of my principal life goals has always been to write and publish a book, another has always been to help others and suffice to say this is the symbiosis of both. What will quickly become noticeable to those who know is the similarity of my conceptual short stories with the legacy of the legendary Milton H. Erickson M.D. He was, is and always will be "The Master" and my single greatest influence. I hope he would approve of my humble efforts. I must also mention the significant influence the genius Richard Bandler has had on upon my work and to a slightly lesser degree the great John Grinder. There are countless other significant others who have affected me and consequentially this text. You are my teachers and are too many to mention; regardless I salute you. Thank you for participating in and thus shaping my model of the world.

INTRODUCTION

I'd like to both welcome and invite you into this book   a book that despite knowing what it is for and knows exactly what it isn't, doesn't exactly know what it is.

Well, rather than accepting any definition imposed upon it by me, or anyone else I suggest that *you* quantify it yourself and eventually *give it its own unique personal context*…if that is okay?

In 1970 Miles Davis and his band played a prolonged 38 minute jazz improvisation at the Isle of Wight Festival to 600,000 amazed spectators; afterwards eager reporters asked what the song was called. In his distinct rasp Davis simply replied "*Call it anything.*"

So in a similar tradition as far as I'm concerned you can call this book anything. You see, rather than a self help book *this is* a help yourself book, and there may be *a key* difference between them!

You may be about to undertake a journey of discovery, expansion and growth. Our interaction will be much like a chemical reaction - that is, a transformational process. In real terms *you* cannot not *be affected by this…* and alas neither can I.

Bear this in mind as I invite you to carefully consider what you are out to read. Some of the content will at times challenge you to adopt a quite different perceptual position. If *you* are *open to suggestion you can* get a lot from this book. Indeed, much of it centres on the principal of *change*…and human beings are generally change resistant.

There is a reason for this which links directly into our neurology, development and evolution as a species – and this my friends can severely impede progressive growth. Therefore, through this lens I would like you to carefully consider this;

If you only ever do what you can do then you will never be more than you are…

So, as *you are, here, now, there, then, wherever* or *whenever* you are, reading this you ought to know at this stage that you are doing so for a reason, are you not? *You* might not *realise* it yet but *your Unconscious Mind* brought you *here*. All will become clear as we progress, but for *now* I would like *you* to *ponder*;

- *Your entire life until this point has been predominantly determined on an unconscious level.*

Now, I know that for many readers the previous statement may not make much sense or seem logical …*yet*…and that's both okay and wholly understandable. *Carefully consider it regardless*. On a surface level those words presuppose a lack of personal control, direction and strategic intent - however as you will discover throughout this book this could not actually be further from the truth. Hang in there, keep an open mind and enjoy the journey!

Hey, wait a minute…why else should I read this book?

Well, I'm glad you asked, that's actually a really good question! It is estimated that when deciding whether or not to invest money, contemplation, comprehension and energy into any book many people unconsciously ask the following questions;

Who cares?

What's the point?

What's in it for me?

Well, firstly let's make it clear from this juncture that unlike some other books of this ilk I do not really offer any unique groundbreaking technique, model or formula as such. I'm not espousing a gimmick or all encompassing method or answer.

In truth there actually is no such thing;

…I am simply expressing my ideas.

That aside however I am of the opinion that you should, could and can care about this book because the whole point is that if a person reads it they may learn some very useful things about themselves, yourself, others, enhance their overall well-being and oh so much more…but only if *you stick around*. The point is that all of this will then afford *you* the opportunity to *expand your horizons* and *attain a greater understanding of who you actually really are, who others actually really are* - and where you are ultimately going.

Amongst other things, this book outlines;

- How to be happier
- The meaning of life
- What you really are
- What your life purpose is
- The true meaning of power
- How to harness your mind
- The unspoken rules of life

- The perspective of infinity
- The truth about beliefs
- How to control physical & emotional pain
- The true nature of trust and confidence
- How to attain what you want
- The reality that is Time Travel

Wait! What?

Oh yes…and so much more.

If all of *this sounds good to you* then that is what's in it for you; expansion. You see, here's the thing;

- *A mind that has been expanded literally never returns to its original size - a phenomenon known as Neuroplasticity.*

So, you now have a decision to make…to read on or not.

Now, I should explain that much of the content of this book is based upon empirical scientific fact. It can therefore be considered as truth or *"It is"* (more on this later). Other parts are based on my own personal hypothesis and experience, along with those of some of the most esteemed and eminent change agents of our time; such as Hypnotherapists, NLP'ers, Psychotherapists, Philosophers, Metaphysicists, Spiritual leaders or random notable others of all ilk.

These can all be classified as *my truth* and *their* collective *truth*. However I must assert that any truth, scientific, medical, psychological, philosophical, spiritual, personal et al is in real terms merely based upon what amounts to what is "the weight of probability" and as such is in real terms constrained by the limits of current knowledge and understanding.

After all, when you think about it, can anything actually ever be proven beyond any shadow of a doubt to be an absolute certainty? Many personal beliefs are held with such emotional conviction that they become held as "certainties", however if a person begins to examine them with objective skepticism reasons why they may actually be false soon become manifest...and that can be a challenging, even uncomfortable experience. For this reason alone many occlude the analysis of personal beliefs.

Regardless, a mindset of true open-mindedness renders many "truths" as fluid and in a perpetual state of flux.

To this end, has it ever struck you how ironic and paradoxical it is that science fiction never seems to change, yet science fact always does...?

Hence, the *only* true universal constant is the continuous flow of *change*, which eternally dictates that, energy aside *nothing is forever*.

This is inclusive of the acceptance of any objective or subjective truth at any time.

Examples;

- *...most ancient cultures (young in actual objective historical terms) completely subscribed to a cosmography that espoused that the Earth was flat. Even today the modern flat earth society boasts some 500 members who refute that we reside upon a cyclical, global planet!*

Any *belief is* a *subjective reality* for those who subscribe to it for as long as it is held...but beware; beliefs are often actual *objective unrealities!*

- ...many 17th and 18th century maps propagated that California was an island and completely separate from mainland USA. This was based on cartographic "fact" – but actually formed from a widely held 16th century European belief!

Carefully consider this - any map is not in literal terms the actual territory.

- ...Classical Newtonian physics, the branch of physics that relates to the behaviour of the macrocosmic was based upon 17th century scientific belief, espousing that atoms were exclusively made of solid mass & were only attracted to each other by gravity. Subsequent, shocking, groundbreaking scientific discovery placed it entirely at odds with the mind bending microcosmic world of Quantum Physics. Yet despite this, classical physics is still often widely favoured by many private educational organisations in the UK.

The frontiers of science are eminently successful – but the *boundaries constantly change*...and, where do they end?

...so, whilst we are on the topic of physics, please be aware that this book is inclusive of snippets of Quantum theory...I know, I know... seriously heavy duty stuff; however I promise you that it is well worth reading. In fact if you are only to consider and grasp one single aspect of this entire book then please <u>ensure</u> it is this content. It is truly mind bending, shocking and if grasped can even be life changing. Most importantly *you* do not need to have an advanced intellectual capacity (whatever that is) to *get it*...I don't and I *do*. Rest assured, so can you.

Now, an admission;

I don't know everything or anything remotely like it. I know nothing about a lot, I know a little about a lot and a lot about a little, that is - not a little about not a lot and the reverse, not the reverse and the opposite of both of that, those, this, these and them...

After all the only real wisdom is that of knowing that you actually know nothing – which I do.

I'd like at this stage to explain the writing style that you will encounter throughout this book.

My intention is to accompany, discuss, persuade, stretch, confuse – who knows, maybe even educate and convince you, the reader. Most importantly, and let's be clear on this… it is all done for one express reason; *to influence …and* thus *empower you.*

So, a question - are *you open to possibility?*

As a practitioner of Neuro-Linguistic Programming (NLP) and a Hypnotherapist I am well aware that there already are a plethora of superb books on the type of topics I'll be covering, mostly written by much cleverer people than me; however there are many others that relate to this that tend to be overly complex, often quite mysterious and therefore generally inaccessible. In my experience this can turn many readers off…including me (I have the tee-shirt and matching underpants!)

Whilst I'm on this topic I should also say at this juncture that simply because I am a practitioner of NLP and a hypnotherapist that I do not blindly subscribe to everything espoused by NLP and hypnotherapeutic theorists …there is a lot of tangential, elitist, irrelevant and even, dare I say completely useless aspects to these.

For this reason alone I intend to keep things as simple as possible, make the material accessible on many levels, and thus engage the single most important aspect of this book…*you.*

You will be exposed to an abundance of *powerful* reframes and techniques in this text. I am an honest person and you should know now, from the outset that I will frequently use many of them on you throughout - in fact this has already started. Just as importantly there are others for *you* to use as you *help yourself*, in your own model of the world.

Look upon them as new and helpful resources to help *you become more*.

Now, a word to the wise; as I alluded to a moment ago many feel the need to manipulate and weave that which is simple and straightforward into that which is intricate and convoluted – they believe on some level that by doing so that they are actually adding value. They often don't and it often doesn't.

I promise you that these techniques are very easy to use. Trust me, they are simplistic, highly effective, have worked for many others and will work for you if *you choose to* take the time *to utilise them*.

Most of all I would really like you to just enjoy this book.

Metaphors, Story Telling and Linguistic word play

Come a little closer, make yourself comfortable…I want to tell you a story about yesterday that will add meaning to today which will shape tomorrow. Here's how it started a long time ago, once upon a time…

Words are eminently powerful in a way that is rarely properly understood below the surface structure; language is one of our most important cognitive filters, it is used to label and quantify all things. My name is *John Glyn Hughes*, but that is not actually who or what I am. That is merely a collection of letters that forms three words. For that reason I am not actually *John Glyn Hughes*…that is just a linguistical representation utilised to quantify what I am, not my reality. Let me explain further…

An example;

Tree – Arbol – Baum – Arbre –Albero - 木 - 树 – Boom - Rakou

All of these collections of letters or symbols form a word; each word is a linguistic representation that quantifies the actual reality of a wide species of generally large, woody plants that have a main stem which develops branches at a distance from the ground from which leaves flower. Bearing in mind that there are currently in the region of 6000 languages in use by human beings, a tree remains a tree regardless of the letters or symbols used to represent it linguistically.

> Your language reveals your thoughts > Your thoughts reveal your interpretation of reality

So, the fact is that a change in language can actually change our perception of the universe. However, one of the problems is that quite often *words* are only able to *reach so deep*. Once this happens there is a requirement to *find a way to reach a much deeper level of meaningful communication…the Unconscious* level.

As the sender and instigator I will use *metaphors, stories* and all manner of *linguistic word play* throughout this book to *connect to different parts of you*, the receiver and responder in a way that no logical reasoning, conversational, debate or argument ever could.

At times you may not understand what is happening as I do so, you might read something and say *"Wait…What? I don't get it!"* and re-read it over again….however that's just fine. Please do so.

I recommend that *you* just *relax* into it and go with the ebb and *flow with the tide and current.*

There is a significant reason for me doing this. Let me explain; the human brain is extremely adept at seeking and making complicated connections, in fact it always try's to do so in all aspects of our subjective, experiential existence;

- *The human brain constantly seeks meaning in all things; it seeks parallels and automatically forms patterns.*

When we hear, see, feel, taste or smell something unfamiliar our brain automatically searches for another thing that we do understand - for the express purpose of establishing a link or drawing a parallel. For this reason, when used properly metaphor, stories and any of a multitude of linguistic techniques can cause what is known as a transderivational search…that is, we instinctively *go inside* and *search for links and parallels*; it is the naturalistic way in which we always want to recognise patterns in all things. However, please always never forget to remember that the actual point of all this is that there is often actually no point. We seek reason and meaning where there is none.

It's part of the madness of the human condition. We often seek, even "demand" explanations for everything because we find that which is unaccountable wholly unacceptable. Often even a bad explanation is considered better than no explanation;

> Something occurs > It has no meaning > We attach a meaning to it > The meaning we attach to it creates our reality > Our reality creates our world > Our world defines our possibilities & impossibilities

I'd like *you* at this embryonic stage of this book to *consider the far reaching connotations of this*. There will be more on this… *later*.

A great source of entertainment, stories are a fantastic way of accounting for real or fictional occurrences or events - everybody loves them for this reason, do you?

However they are so much more than this.

Stories are incredibly *useful* for *teaching* through the introduction of new ideas or illustrating different points…they can make a complex reality much easier to understand. They can be challenging, enlightening… they can be scary, emotional, comforting and so much more. *Stories* can *reach* people, *engage* them and *hold* their *attention* in a way that mere facts cannot. Stories have been used throughout human history to pass information down from generation to generation… and thus serve as a bridge through the ages. They can allow us to understand the past, gain perspective in the here and now and give us a way to connect with and shape the future.

They provide metaphors that we can assimilate and carry with us throughout our lives.

A former colleague of mine once observed;

"Why do you always talk in metaphorical terms" – to which I replied, "It's because I am drawn to metaphors as a bear is drawn to the woods when it needs the toilet!"

Metaphors are analogies for metaphors, and they allow us to draw parallels between normally unrelated things. They allow us to explain a situation by referencing another one.

They put things into perspective and enable us to see things in a new light…they can even shape perceptions.

People often *feel more comfortable* describing a situation as a metaphor than they would when using a literal description. For these reasons *metaphorical stories are* much more *meaningful and powerful* than they appear at a cursory glance. They allow others to *see things from a different point of view*…and are thus a catalyst for teaching, persuasion and growth.

I will use metaphorical stories at times throughout this book. Most are actually completely factual, others are fictional…some are both or neither.

These stories are absolutely ripe with multi layered meanings within meanings; *you* may need to *read them several times*, and *contemplate them* on a higher level before *gaining* an *understanding* of *their true* hidden *message*.

There is much to not be not learnt from these.

The use of linguistics and syntax in this book will consist of a myriad of techniques; *you* don't need to *understand* how or what *I* am doing, suffice to say that the why is purely that of *benevolence* - I am doing it *to help you*, as this is my primary personal value and life purpose. *Language* will often be precisely vague in the way that it is tailored throughout to *reach you on the deepest level* of *your unconscious*, which incidentally *is always listening*.

Unconventionally, for a piece of written literature I consider prescriptive grammar to be much less important than the semantics; for it is the semantics that will determine how *you process* and compute *the content within* what is the realm of neuro-linguistics. This will make *this book* more *meaningful*.

Now, at this point if you regard all of this as pointless, arbitrary and fanciful... then you are absolutely right. Equally if *you consider all of this to be intriguing, engaging and curious* then you are absolutely right.

You see, as I have already alluded - the reality is that *you* actually *create your own reality*; this will become apparent on our journey together if *you choose to read on...*

In essence, this book is a *mind to mind communication* between you and me.

After all neither of us are physically sitting together looking at, able to touch and talk to each other. My cognitive function has promulgated these words via an incredibly complex symbiosis which combines a neurological, physiological and technological process…and yours perceives them in an equally elaborate way. Linguists who adhere to the laws of linguistics assert that the written word is not language, it cannot be as it is unspoken…but (cough, cough) oh contraire. They miss one crucial and quite critical point;

- *As you read that which is written your internal voice actually verbalises the text inside.*

Have *you* just *noticed* that *you are doing that*? You always have and always do – everyone does. The written word is thus almost always an auditory phenomenon! And because of this *you* will *paint* imaginary *images, holograms* or *pictures in your head* and you will attach *feelings* to all that which you perceive. Words are also capable of invoking smells and tastes. I remember cutting a lemon; the overwhelming clean, fresh citrus fragrance that filled the air. I recall licking the juice that had dripped onto my fingers …the memory of the overwhelming flavour as I licked my fingers is absolutely unforgettable!

All of this cognitive activity will *bring this book to life…inside!* In this way the experience will become visceral… immersive

Have you considered this before? Furthermore you should know at this stage that *you* actually *have utter and complete control of* these *internal processes* that have *always* accompanied you. In fact *they are you*. Oh, and by the by I would like to you to understand this…all of this is significantly impactive upon your personal day to day well-being!

Your unconscious mind is here and *can hear what* you and *I say*. Each and both of you should keep that in mind.

Oh, and just one further recommendation; if you have a printed version of this book then please use a highlighter pen to outline any aspects of the text that you find interesting, useful, confusing, stupid or otherwise. As a book lover I used to be precious about defacing the text of even my less favoured titles; only to later discover that many people find *this a very useful practice…*

If it's right to do so then its right, unless it is wrong…and if wrong is right then right is wrong and that's right and not wrong! It's that simple, right?

And so, without further ado, become comfortable and let's *you, your internal voice and I* begin…

1 LIFE

Memento Mori…you are going to die.

In fact you are dying right now.

I've been dying to tell you that. Okay, I concede that it's perhaps not *the greatest way to open the opening chapter* of any book, especially if the chapter is entitled "life" but, hey…don't shoot the messenger! I'm just putting it out there. There is of course a valid reason for this, as shall become apparent. You see, to discuss life and your Life Purpose we actually do need to discuss death - because it's an important aspect of it!

You are a bespoke, cybernetic, biological, sentient universal system that comprises an intriguing symbiosis of sub atomic particles and non physical consciousness; to paraphrase, *you are* combined of *Mind and Body*. In the simplest of terms you are Energy.

In fact, allow me to further quantify *you* as *a* composite *Quantum Mechanical device*, and consequentially are not only an integral part of the universe…*you inexorably are the universe.*

- *Energy can never cease, it can only change form and transpose. You are a spiritual life force having a human experience.*

Please re-read that last sentence and consider the implications. All of this may or may not have your head in a spin at this point, if it doesn't, then great and if it does, then great; it just is regardless ...

Now, where was I? Ah, yes, death. As a species we do like to brand everything. Think about it, we do it to our livestock…and we do it to ourselves (Nike, Adidas, Levis, Rolex anyone?) and as a result death can be loosely branded as the termination of the biological function of any living organism. As such it forms a vital part of the physiological life cycle – and is consequentially equally as important as conception, development, birth, growth, maturity, decay, expiration, conception, development, birth growth, maturity, decay, expiration…and so on and so forth.

Be that as it may the human psyche, at least on a surface level is generally averse to the consideration of death, or non-existence, and as a result it tends to be a bit of a conversation killer. The disinclination to face death is firmly implanted within us on the deepest level; we are neurologically hardwired to survive, procreate and nurture, thus ensuring the ongoing cyclical replication of our species.

However if, like Dorothy, the Tin man, the Cowardly Lion, the Scarecrow and Toto you snap out of your comfortable inertia, push the curtains aside and take a peek back stage (and why wouldn't you?) it becomes blatantly apparent that as a species we are completely and utterly obsessed with the creation of life…that is, sex - or if you prefer a slightly more romantic and polite terminology, the persistent, often unconscious urge to procreate. In fact it is the only thing that supersedes our sense of importance! If you are unsure or unconvinced of this at this point then consider just one small example of this - the way in which we have historically surrounded ourselves on a subliminal level with man made phallic objectification;

- *Skyscrapers – the BIGGER the better.*
- *Guns (a barrel that ejaculates bullets…okay!)*
- *Church steeples*
- *Towers (Jacobs, Eiffel, Blackpool, Trump…hmmm!)*
- *Monuments*
- *Obelisks*
- *Pyramids*
- *Skittles (Bowling pins)*
- *Cigars*
- *Lipstick*
- *Many pens (seriously, take a look at some of them)*
- *Sauce bottles that dispense fluid when squeezed…*

Think about it. The list could go on and on and on…

Now, taken into this context consider the utterly despicable and devastating attacks that took place upon the Twin Towers in NYC on September 11, 2001. Apart from the obvious emotional abreaction that resonated around the world following this vile deed, *think about the deeply unconscious metaphorical symbolism* of such a destructive, violent annihilation upon not only one, but TWO of the worlds most powerful and proud tribes most famous of landmark phallic symbols.

- *Powerful phallic symbols associated with the tribes power, wealth, prowess and fertility…reduced, albeit temporarily to being associated with an efficacious form of defeat, destruction and violent death of a large number of fellow tribal members by an opposing enemy tribe.*

But the crux is that despite tribalism we are actually one species and are thus irrevocably connected; thus the acts of destruction and violence that we impose upon others equate in the grand scheme of things to acts of destruction and violence upon us.

Really *take a few moments to think about this...*

Quite shocking isn't it.

Anyway, as I was saying before I interrupted me the whole point of sex is to spread the seed and expand the tribe in an evolutionary continuum. This is the reason for all of our base feelings of pride, preening, attraction, love, lust, joy, nurturing, protectiveness, tribalism, jealousy, anger...anxiety and fear. It is at the root of all of our actions. Furthermore, once life has been created and nurtured the preservation of it assumes paramount importance within all of the societies of the human race. In an indirect way this is often utilised by the "great and the good" as emotional leverage to manipulate the *Untere Schicht* to rally under the banner for some covert agenda, take up arms and make war upon enemy tribes...who incidentally have been manipulated likewise for an equal and opposite covert agenda! Do *you catch my drift?*

This aside, *you* can *realise now* this preservation of *life* is blatantly apparent in all walks of life. We seek to delay the inevitable because it is so unpalatable. This is the very reason why, in many cases in western society, those elderly hospital patients who are in the final painful stages of life will have their remaining time extended for *as long as possible* by any means, artificial or otherwise, rather than allowing them to naturally, or unnaturally just slip away;

Princey Boy

I found him as a wild rebellious mongrel. Untamable and free I tamed him with a simple high value treat; a bag of cooked sausages in my pocket which meant he never left my side. Near the end as I lay by my terminally ill pet dog his big brown eyes met my big brown eyes...and they pled for blessed relief.

Princey boy had suffered in agony for weeks. He knew that I knew that the only humane thing left to do now was the final act of human kindness, which for him I did...because I loved him so.

...and yet, I wondered why it was considered inhumane to do the same humane act for a human?

Now, because of all of this we just don't like to *talk about death* much...however shrinking away from it is actually unhealthy. Indeed, it is a truism that some things are better left unsaid - however I personally am of the opinion that *sometimes* we actually should *take the time to speak about the unspoken,* which I do and will;

Fear of the unknown

A girl I knew liked to think about things. She did a lot of that in the privacy of her head. She wasn't particularly talkative, but said a lot.

She told me she wanted to ask me about her fear of death as it was causing her concern. I told her to ask away whenever she liked. She was young, exceptionally bright, attractive, and very healthy. She explained that she thought a lot about it and the more she thought about it the more she became fearful, anxious and frightened.

I asked her what scared her about it and she emphatically replied "Fear of the unknown!" I said "Well, what did it feel like when you were dead before?" ...which seemed to stop her right there, where she was, in her tracks. After a long pause and a not unconfused period of introspection she replied "...Sorry? What on earth do you mean???"...to which I explained "Well, before you were born you were dead, how did it feel then?"

She thought about that a lot because she liked to think about things a lot and became less fearful, anxious and frightened to be dead…

She was open to suggestion and liked to think about things.

Human beings are great at learning things then forgetting them – we only remember that which we use! As a result we do *know a lot* and then tend to forget what we know. It's not what we know that we don't know that causes us problems in life…it's what we don't know that we know. Sometimes a change of perspective or way of looking at something can prove to be an absolute revelation. This is known in NLP as Reframing; you'll notice me doing this a lot as we proceed.

The deep dark lake

Four men are fishing for fish in the middle of a deep dark lake on a small boat. Suddenly a freak wave upturns the boat and all four men are pitched into the watery water. Their shouts for help go unheard and one by one by one by one they gradually sink to the bottom of the deep dark lake never to be seen again…yet not one single man got wet.

How can that be possible?

Well, it's actually quite simple - all four men were married!

It's all about perspective, perspective, perspective. If *you change the way that you look at things*, then the things that *you* look at *change!* If you look at things differently then *you can do things differently…*

That watery riddle also reminds me of an interesting case that I knew but had forgotten.

So whilst I'm *a rocking and a rolling* here is;

The water baby

A mature man came to see me because he was terrified of water, so terrified that he had never been able to learn how to swim. He was a man of the world who liked to talk a lot. Such was his fear he explained that he couldn't enter the sea or even a swimming bath to a depth any deeper than that of his knees. This caused him much concern and feelings of angst as he felt that as a mature, professional man of the world with much to say he should not live with feelings of fear of water! I stated that it must have been difficult to come to grips with such feelings, and that it must have felt like a really heavy weight on his shoulders. He agreed to agree with how I felt about how he felt!!

Now, I only knew that he had managed to stand up to his knees in water, but asked him if he had ever been able to submerge his thighs, waist, torso, chest, neck, chin, head and hair under water.

He visibly shuddered at the thought and emphatically said "No, never. I have never done that and just could not ever conceive of doing that!"

I told him that he was wrong and that he was wrong.

I then asked him what he was not thinking about when he was thinking about being scared of water, which caused him to stop right there in his tracks and think. I then asked him how he had managed when he used to live underwater... and for some reason he became bewildered.

After a short pause and the briefest moment of pupillary expansion he stated "...I'm sorry? I don't understand. I have never lived underwater!!"

...The penny finally dropped when I replied; "Really? Have you forgotten that you lived underwater for 9 months...did you not?"

Choosing to overcome his fearful feelings, he went on to enjoy swimming lessons. He came to terms with the fact that he had forgotten that he had actually once been an amniotic water baby...

We are only born with one fear...that of loud noises; all others are learnt. That's a lot of learning and we do so very comprehensively.

So, from the moment of conception we physically undertake the inception of living...and thus we begin to die and become fearful, and some are more proficient at it than others. We are from that point, in real terms on a literal collapsing timeframe.

It is true that *life is* extremely unpredictable, and often not what we would ideally like it to be, but it is *precious* nonetheless and we should *live it*. Life will often bring each person pain, however it is the responsibility of the person to *create* their own *Joie de Vie*. After all everyone dies, but not everyone lives.

Nobody knows how long they will have, but consider this;

- *It's what you do with your time that makes the difference.*

Taid

David committed suicide when I was a small boy. He had suffered from depression for such a long time. He had repeatedly begged his doctor for help once he had realised that he felt suicidal and that he could no longer take the chance of acquiescing to an important social norm of life in rural north Wales; the unspoken rule stipulated that talking about emotions and mental health was utterly taboo. It was 1971 after all, and people just didn't do that, let alone a working class mans man.

He took the decision to hang himself after being told to snap out of it once too often… he found that he had lost the know how.

The laws of causality dictate that any action has an equal and opposite reaction – therefore the after effects have been deeply felt for generations. More than one of his family members subsequently deduced that such a mental state must be genetically hereditary, and therefore was inescapable - so they chose to induce similar said depressive thought processes, went away and practiced a lot and became really good at doing it…

That was one parting gift I'm certain Taid would not have wished to bequeath.

My grandmother coped well. There is a pervasive undercurrent that hints that women are society's weak minority; when in fact they are actually society's strong majority.

As a wise man once said… half of my ancestors were women.

In truth most human beings spend most of their time living in a reactionary state of emotional unease; ranging from mild worries to extreme suffering. Most of us sit at the lower end of the scale, experiencing such issues as low self esteem or insecurities based upon body image and such like. As a consequence most people can be classified as *Neurotic* to some degree, and as such never quite feel good enough inside (that's right – *it's not just you in touch with those feelings!*)

By the way, please do not consider being classified as having Neurotic tendencies to be a slight upon your good name, it should not be considered as an insult. The alternative psychological archetypes are to be classified as having Psychopathic and Sociopathic tendencies. This is somewhat less than *awesome*. More on this …*later*

Often built upon a foundation of anxiety and stress, depression is a response to what will have been an increasing inability to cope with negative thinking which has led to persistent feelings of sadness. It can sit at a point slightly higher up the scale, and in some extreme cases leads to nervous breakdown and even suicide. Such depressive emotional states are born of negative thoughts and are much like any other habitual behaviour (habit or addiction if you prefer) – and as such its best that *you do yourself a favour* and are proactive in choosing to *take all appropriate action* to *kick that shit to the kerb* my friends. Suicide is at the most extreme end of the scale and such a particularly painful event – I have had to deal with it more than once so feel somewhat qualified to quantify;

- *Suicide is a <u>permanent</u> solution to a <u>temporary</u> problem.*

Now, to the point – and this may be an extreme example, but my Welsh grandfather lost sight of his *life purpose* and therefore could see no purpose. In any case, it is true that I was unfortunate enough to lose a grandfather - but at least was fortunate enough to have, and be grateful for another.

When life comes crashing down it can be helpful to *take a good look at that which remains*, make the best of it ...*and move on towards what will be.*

At this juncture you should know that the author is well qualified to make comment due to the fact I have suffered some *terrible hardships in life* and have known much physical and emotional *pain and trauma*. I won't bore you with the details suffice to say that I surmounted them all by never letting go of a vision of better things to come; by understanding that *all* suffering *must pass*.

You can after all *choose your attitude* in any of life's circumstances – this is an important human freedom, this is Stoicism. Stoicism does not merely hinge on the ability to endure and persevere…it enables. It enables for each and every adversity to be manipulated to advantage. In this way that which impedes action advances action.

Know that the best thing about *the past* is that it *is over*. More on depression and my aunties uncles Scottish brother …*later*

Anyway, all of this aside, I personally *really enjoy living* on this planet, so I have decided that *dying is the last thing* I intend *to do so to* ensure long life I have developed a clever strategy; to *wake up every morning*

… So I have a hard lumpy mattress and drink a large glass of milk before going to bed every night…

Time and the meaning of life

Now, it takes an awful lot to annoy me, but if you were to ask me to identify something that does, I would reply; *"I hate people who answer questions with another question…how about you?"*

So, my question to you and it is a hugely significant one at this point in proceedings is;

- *What is your life purpose?*

If you know what it is then what are you doing to work towards it in the time that you have been allocated?

If you don't know what it is then what are you doing to work towards finding out what it is in the time that you have been allocated?

Now, I know a thing or two about time because *I'm a time traveler*.

Wait!! What??

Yes, that's right you read that correctly. I'm a time traveler...you see, I'm *from* the past, *at* the present and am going *to* the future (at least to some degree) – and so are you. We are all travelling through time. Have you ever considered that? Let's explore;

Time is seemingly infinite, but it's fair to assert that our physical allocation is most certainly finite.

Those much cleverer than the author such as Physicians and Mathematicians classify time as the fourth dimension; nonetheless its predominant efficacy as a way of measuring events in an ordered fashion from the past, to the present and into the future is predominant. We arrange the past and the future as *memories* – an integral component of the mind filtration system. In NLP this is the Timeline, and through the use of *Timeline work* we can make some *incredibly* efficacious and *potent improvements* to human wellness.

This apart, in its simplest form time can consequentially be harnessed to codify and measure the durations between lifetime events and also the intervals that intersperse them. We all do this do we not? Yet still...*it is more than this.*

When do your life experiences actually take place? I would appreciate it if you could take some time to think on this concept; your life happens here... *now!* Despite actually being from the past I *realise that all thinking about the past happens at the present moment,* all thinking about the future happens at the present moment;

- *All time is actually now. The past happened now, now is happening now and the future will be in the now at that point in time when it arrives …which it now has and soon now will again…now…and again…now.*

All of our *Memories* of the past and of the future are very real and have a major impact upon our lives because they correlate to our present emotional state. Most human beings devote an incredible amount of energy to these realities, it is an unfortunate part of the madness of our species – but they are only real in the sense that they are stored in our minds as thoughts. Your past does not need to equate to your present or future.

You see, Time is an absolutely fundamental dimensional part of our subjective (and therefore objective) structured existence… indefinite, infinite, unlimited and often paradoxical. We all experience time, manipulate it, code it, fight it, organise and deal with it in an individualistically subjective way; it is a quintessential part of our existence…and *time* is absolutely *the single greatest, most valuable resource* of all…

National Service

Last week, my father told me about something that had happened when he was sitting on a bench reading in the shade, in the army in North Africa in 1956 when it was 92 degrees, and his friend told him afterwards that his dads brothers wife had told him to tell her sister this;

"Time flies when you're having fun, so how long will you remember this?"

It was the 7th April, 1956 at 1308hrs, he was sitting on a wooden bench reading in the shade in North Africa and it was 92 degrees. His friend talked to him, time has flown and he has remembered…

He told me that it only seemed like yesterday.

Isn't it odd that time speeds up as we age? It is true that we begin to underestimate intervals of time as we become older. I *remember being 10 years old* and each day seemed to last forever.

Those things that I yearned for, such as the school bell, Starsky & Hutch and birthday and Christmas presents seemed to take forever to arrive – yet now weeks, months and even years are now slipping through my fingers and I am constantly asking *"Where the hell has all the time gone?"* Now this can, at least in part be related to the neurological effects of the lowering of *Dopaminergic* levels in relation to the *Neo-cortex* and *Hippocampus* regions of the aging brain– but it is also arguably related to a growing theory that relates the humanistic perception of the passage of time to statistical percentages.

Allow me to explain;

One day to a 10 year old child (like I was *now*) is approximately 1-4,000th of their lifetime, whereas a day to a 55 year old adult (like I will be when I am *now*) is approximately 1-20,000th of their life.

This theory is therefore linked to the perception of time being associated with the proportionality of a person's lifetime. It can therefore be useful when explaining why an average day would then consequentially appear to be longer to a 10 year old child. In this way a 20 year old adult will experience an average day as being 2 x as experientially fast as a 5 year old child – and an 80 year old adults day will experientially pass 4 x faster than a 20 year old adult…ergo, an 80year olds day would be 8 x quicker than a 5 year old Childs.

Wow! Have a *think about that* for a few moments.

Anyway, despite being a tad tangential (*I am prone to wondering*), as the single greatest resource available to us Time is worth pondering…*know what I mean?* It's worth making the time to *make peace with your past* or it will disrupt your present, time is after all a great healer and heals all…if *you give it time.*

Life is made of time, so let's get back on track *now* and *return to Life* and expand on this just a little further.

I have actually been asked *"What is the meaning of life?"* quite a few times; in fact it seems to be generally considered as one of those *impossible* to explain esoteric obscurities - a deeply elusive, expansive and infinitely divine existential secret or conundrum. The question has usually been posed to me as some sort of *"Aha! Now get out of this one!"* type puzzle…which of course puzzles me not because it isn't. As with many of universal truths, the answer is simplicity in itself,

- *The meaning of life is the things that give meaning to your life*

There is no overarching, singular life meaning that applies to all subjective human experiential system; no simple, single way. For me, each subjective human life form will determine their applicable subjective life meanings.

There is no way…only ways. So, what way gives your life meaning?

Establishing your life purpose

Now, how then do you discover your life purpose? Well, firstly let's quantify it for what it actually is.

Your life purpose is not an outcome or goal, it is not your current or future set of responsibilities, it is not your employment, nor your status or position...*it is the actual reason for your existence!*

If you are now thinking *"Whoa, that's pretty deep!"* then, *helloooo*...welcome to this book, lie down on the couch and tell me all about your childhood! I would like at this point to *outline* two of the many *ways* that can *enable* towards uncovering your *life purpose*; the first can be done strategically via a simplistic sequential process.

Method 1 - You should;

- *Accept yourself*...but never sell yourself short! This is more difficult than you may think because to do so you need to often swim against the tide of your environment, significant others, education and culture...which has stipulated that which you should either conform to or aspire to be - or not. <u>Much of this has been a lie</u>. Has it ever been explained to you that *you are* as *good* as you are and can *be as good as you want to be*? Self obsession is extremely unhealthy but a basic form of *self love is absolutely essential*; you cannot truly *love others* unless *you* first truly *love yourself*...after all *perception is projection*. You are unique and incomparable, there never has been, or ever will be another you. *You have virtually got unlimited potential...*

- *Take the time to realise your talents, gifts and personal genius.* You have undoubtedly been gifted with many specific skills, capabilities and talents that will actually give you all of the resources that you need to meet your life purpose. *Everybody does.* The first step towards discovering what your life purpose is lies in personally *recognising*, and *validating these gifts*. We all have them; they usually come naturally to us - importantly they can then be further refined, developed and honed to allow us to grow and become more. Taking them for granted is a major error that many make. The more *you become* the *greater* your capability to fulfill your life purpose. *(*See the "Happiness" chapter for more on this)*

- *Be open to Change, Experience ... and be Patient.* Many people resist change and reside within the constraints of acceptance and *being comfortable*. Comfort is a truly wonderful thing in the proper context- but can also be inhibitive and preventive with reference to the attainment of that which is greater. Be assured, the Universe has a way of shaking the tree and forcing your hand if the leaves on your branches don't *blow in the flow of the winds of change*. Furthermore, there is often no substitute for experience - you cannot not, not put an old head on young shoulders. So, *you* simply may not *be ready to know your life purpose* yet. In fact, *you* may not *identify* or *begin* to *fulfill your life purpose* until you have lived much of it…I didn't realise mine until I was almost 45 years old. If this is the case for you then *you* wont *have* wasted *time*, it has just taken time! *You have just been maturing emotionally, spiritually* and *psychologically* in preparation.

- *Always do your best regardless of circumstance.* You might be frustrated through the feeling that you are not currently fulfilling your life purpose; however in the meantime, *always do your best* in all things. *You are* likely to be *learning new skills* and *gaining valuable experience* that will become very pertinent *in ways that you* cannot possibly currently *imagine*. This is the principal of the "Big Picture". Set high standards in all things and your resultant actions will not be in vain. The *creative forces* that are beyond our comprehension always *utilise positive energy*…

- *Do the things that you naturally enjoy.* Ask yourself - *"Is there anything that I would do even if I wasn't paid to do it?"* The answer will probably give you a big clue as to what your life purpose is. This will likely be *something* that *you just naturally love* doing. My primary life purpose, and an important part of my ethos is to help others as much as possible; I achieve this through being empathic, kind, and helpful (usually!). My practice of therapy, coaching, training, writing (and any other countless ways) gives me the platform to do so. This is *my calling* and it *gives me tremendous fulfilment*; what's yours?

- **Consider how you are serving others.** Make no mistake; your life purpose will be likely to *contribute towards making the world a better place*. If you are raising a family then you are nurturing individuals who will eventually take the baton on from you as they *work towards blessing and enhancing the lives of others*. If you are a writer, musician, artist or actor then you are creating art forms for others to behold. If *you* are a teacher then *you* are passing on the gift of learning and thus *are a catalyst for Neuroplasticity*…if you are a bricklayer you are constructing modern day caves to allow modern day cavemen and their modern day cave family to shelter from modern day sabre tooth tigers…nice!

Method 2 – is a simple naturalistic, holistic way;

Find a blank piece of paper & pen, open up a new word processing screen on your computer (or device), or arm yourself with a blank flip chart page and a marker pen.

- Write at the top of the page *"What is my true life purpose?"*

- Now take a few seconds, or as long as it takes to *empty and still your mind*. Just let thoughts drift by like cognitive clouds in your cognitive sky as you do this. Observe them dispassionately from a detached perspective. This can be achieved through simply allowing your eyes to fixate and focus upon something, a point on the wall… and then allowing them to go out of focus; after a few minutes notice the your peripheral vision actually begins to expand and the *things out there come into focus*...Pay more attention to the periphery than the spot you are staring at.

- Once the time feels right ponder the question you have posed, and when you are ready simply write an answer...any answer. It shouldn't be filtered through any critical conscious process, be expansive, clever or a long sentence or passage of words. Just trust what bobbles to the surface of your mind.

- If the answer doesn't seem to be quite right then repeat the process again and again until the answer does seem right.

And it is as simple as that. Any answers that do not seem to fit can usually be quantified as having come from some area of the surface level of your mind, or from some memory, experience, attitude or decision. The answer that seems just right will appear to have come from an entirely different source altogether.

That's because it has!

The key unwritten rules of life

I would like to complete this bite size segment of this chapter by identifying three simple rules of life that, if comprehended, ingested, known and understood will prevent much mental perturbation, exasperation, frustration and misinterpretation of life events and interpersonal relationships.

The unwritten key rules of life once written are no longer unwritten, but have become written and consist of;

- *Life is not fair.* There is the way things should be, and the way things are. It is that simple. *What are you going to do about it?* People fascinate and interest me, and I am curious about others. One thing that never ceases to amaze me is how many people just seem totally unable to accept this unwritten but absolute rule. They torture themselves in the process and are consequentially fighting the perpetual flow and thus always swimming upstream, cast in the role of *victim*. This causes dissatisfaction and unease. Take a look at newspaper letters pages to find superb daily illustrations of this phenomenon.

- *People will let you down.* If you look back on your life and count how many <u>true</u> friends that you have accumulated you will be doing well to do so on the fingers of one hand. I always chuckle inwardly when I hear others discussing their 2,545 Facebook friends or Twitter followers. Yes, you will amass many, many casual friends, acquaintances and associates during your journey – a word to the wise, even those whom you have counted upon the fingers of one hand will have let you down from time to time….never mind the other 2, 540. Real friends are easily identifiable; they can be found standing by your side helping you to salvage that worth recovering from the debris of your lightening struck tower.

- *The goalposts will change.* They do and they will. Expect the unexpected. For just one prime example cast your mind back to the *"Credit Crunch"*, itself a simple, yet clever reframe – it is after all much more palatable and easier to swallow than *"Global Bankruptcy"*, which it inevitably was and continues at this time of writing to be. In 2008 the goal posts changed and many major players suddenly became an overnight bust. Isn't it strange however that the subsequent *"Austerity"* measures imposed upon the working classes and poorest elements of the worlds societies seem to be facilitating for the insanely wealthy to become yet more insanely wealthy? Oh, and by the way have you given any thought to the role that psychopaths, and to a lesser extent Sociopaths are playing in all of this? *You should…*

So, to paraphrase these rules; *it isn't, they will* (no matter how much they love or care for you, or otherwise) *and they will*. Apply these rules to all aspects of life, allow for and expect the unexpected and you will be less likely to be caught off balance and constantly find yourself pushing invisible pins into yourself or giving yourself proverbial Chinese burns on a daily basis.

To summarise, it is probably best to *avoid idealism* as you cruise your way down the winding dual carriage of life…it just leads to disappointment, annoyance and the unavoidable, eventual decline into cynicism and bitterness. With this in mind I always taught my eldest daughter this when teaching her to drive;

"As soon as you open the door, take a seat, apply your seatbelt, check your mirrors, start the engine, engage first gear, remove the handbrake, depress the accelerator and leave the safety of the driveway know that every other driver that you are about to encounter on your journey …is a complete idiot"

I always found that *this mindset prevents much anger, swearing, disappointment* and head scratching…

Beliefs

What do you believe? Every question contains linguistical presuppositions. It cannot not; for example the above question presupposes that you are (identity), you are reading the question (behaviour), you can believe (capability) and that you are believing (behaviour). However, have you ever considered that any belief can be a real reality or a real unreality? Read on.

For your pleasure you might contemplate this little riddle;

It is,

It is not,

It might be,

What is It?

The answer, of course is a *belief*! With this in mind I'd like you to process the following context with regard beliefs - *It is, It isn't …or you don't know*. Let me explain;

If *It* can be empirically proven then *It Is (real reality)*. *If It can be empirically proven that it is not then It Isn't (unreal reality). If It can not empirically prove that It Is or that It Isn't then…you don't know (unproven reality).*

Believe it (sorry) or not many beliefs fall into the *"you don't know"* category. A belief is subjectively real for as long as it is held – but is objectively either a real reality an unreal reality…or an unproven reality. I appreciate at this juncture that all of this may be a bit of a head scratcher, however beginning to think in alternative ways is a pivotal part of what this book is all about. To assist you I have developed a very simplistic filter to apply in your daily life when listening to others, who will undoubtedly frequently include what can be very revealing belief statements in their day to day verbal communications.

The following is my own conceptual personal belief filtration model. I'm not sure if there is anything else out there like it – if there is then its purely coincidental...because this is mine and now it is yours;

It Is (real reality)

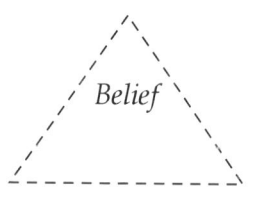

Belief

It Isn't (unreal reality)   *Don't Know (unproven reality)*

In practical terms, from this juncture I'd like you to start utilising the model. Use it when listening to others as they lay bare their belief statements. People do actually verbalise them all the time! It is useful to filter them through this simple model.

So whilst we are discussing the beliefs of others let's talk about you. The more *you think about the following* the more *you* can *understand it.* So;

Whatever your own personal, religious, metaphysical or philosophical beliefs on the continuum of life, death, the *afterlife*, the *afterdeath, the lifeafter or the deathafter* you are entitled to them. It is *absolutely* your prerogative to believe whatever you want. Your beliefs are *absolutely* yours for as long as you choose to believe them. This of course extends to any other belief that you have subscribed to in any aspect of your subjective living experience thus far. You should know at this juncture that beliefs are *incredibly powerful* in ways that are often wholly misunderstood – they play a huge role in the way in which we have lived, are living and in how we manipulate our future circumstances. Still unconvinced? Then, contemplate the following mass held beliefs;

- *"Everything happens for a reason"* – Really? Well, it is impossible to prove or disprove…so we don't know – but it is all encompassing and thus serves as a rationale to all rational responses to it, supportive or otherwise!
- *"I can't do that because I'm not good at … (insert)"* – Really? When did you decide that? Can you not become good or at least better at doing anything? Regardless of whether you think you can or think you cant you are right. You might be best avoiding limiting self fulfilling prophecies.
- *"No pain – no gain"* – Really? Oh, contraire….there can be much to gain without the need to attract discomfort & suffering dear reader.
- *"Money is the root of all evil"* – Really? Money can be used to affect positivity, generosity and benevolence on a significant world scale. Money is <u>not</u> evil…human misuse of money can be!
- *"God has a plan for each and us all!"* – Really? Well, maybe, maybe not…it can be neither proven nor disproven so we don't actually know. Those of a religious persuasion will assert that due to faith no proof is required; agnostics will assert that blind faith is misplaced faith…

The thing is this; two people with polar opposite beliefs will tend to witness the exact same event…but both believe that it proves and supports their individual position. Indeed this is known as *Confirmation Bias;* a cognitive bias evidenced by a flawed subjective inductive reasoning which only serves to confirm a belief - usually through the prejudiced interpretation of events.

- *Reframe = all beliefs only serve to mitigate for uncertainty and thus …fear.*

Anyway, *you get what you focus on*, so if you imagine a future reality that you can really believe in you will have subscribed to it on an unconscious level, and are subsequently much more likely to create it as your future reality. This is called *Goal Setting*, is proactively direction driven and as such *"It is"*.

This is great if you have the wherewithal to be able to subscribe to empowering beliefs, however if your beliefs are restricting or disempowering you, or causing some other negative or debilitating impact upon your well-being or life journey I would strongly suggest that you give serious consideration to choosing to start believing something else…in fact *anything else*. Many beliefs are deeply implanted into us; much like seeds into the deep warm earth of our *Unconscious Minds* during the earliest formative, imprint period of our lives. Crucially this often happens when our critical filtering faculty is either not present or fully developed, usually before puberty. They then shape our thoughts, perceptions, realities and drive the programs or patterns that we run; our behaviours. Once a belief is strongly accepted a person will then continually reinforce it by recognising every life event that supports it…like a continual self fulfilling prophecy.

- *Many of our beliefs are deeply embedded within our unconscious mind and dictate our lives…therefore if you want to change your reality you need to change your beliefs*

For this reason you should <u>*be very careful*</u> about what *you* believe. Your beliefs become your realities.

We cannot not communicate, and as a result many of our beliefs are displayed for all to see; however, a great many remain hidden, underlying and therefore unseen.

In Control

A structured, controlled mature lady called me several times, anxiously seeking to see me for a problem that was getting too much. When she finally arrived her body language told me that she didn't want to tell me anything.

She announced that she had acted in haste, her problem had suddenly cleared up and that she did not require treatment. In the process she inadvertently told me she hadn't, it hadn't and that she did. The harder she tried not to reveal anything the more revealing she became.

She left after five minutes having terminated her request, happy that she was not not in control and had told me nothing, which she had not...

It would serve you well to *bear this in mind* when dealing with others...even those whom you think you know intimately. There is always much on show, however the exact rationale is often hard to discern. If you were able to actually gain full insight into all of their deepest beliefs, those located well beneath the surface, you may well be very surprised at what you would find. In fact, you might be astounded at what some people actually believe;

The Garden of beliefs

I helped a young stable man from an old unstable background with his anxiety. He sent a young man who had a useful knack for overcoming challenges in what had often been a challenging life to see me. He seemed to meet them with courage and an assured, quiet confidence that was admirable. This had led to some notable achievements, all of which done with an admirable humility and a self possessed kind of air... it seemed to surround him like an invisible aura.

His successes were however actually beginning to cause him problems because the struggle to stay the best is a much harder one than the struggle to become the best - but that's another story...

Anyway, as I am interested and curious in interesting and curious people, which everyone is, this interested me, so I decided to do a bit of gentle digging in the flower bed of his garden of beliefs.

I enquired as to the secret of his strategy for success, to which he was gracious enough to confide;

"I know that this sounds insane, and that others would think me mad, but I draw on the strength given to me by the invisible Native American that looks after me. He has always been with me.... he is strong, proud, fierce yet noble. A warrior and a holy man, he is wise and gives me his strength in times of need. I know he is always with me... I cannot fail!"

...What an effective strategy! When the harvest offered up by the garden of beliefs is ripe you do indeed reap what you sow...

The above case illustrates the way in which *beliefs can be empowering*, benevolent and incredibly useful. The flip side however is the opposite, not the opposite and the reverse of this, these, those and that.

We will revisit beliefs a little more later on in this book, but suffice to say at this juncture *each and both of you* need to *know* that *beliefs* are one of the most overarching parts of our unconscious mind filtering system. Any belief is actually either an objective real *reality*, an objective real *unreality*...or a subjective real *reality* or a subjective real *unreality*.

I now formally invite you to *Re-frame* the concept of beliefs for all time;

- *Beliefs can be defined as Emotionally Based Opinions.*

And there it is, right there…the introduction of that *emotional* aspect tends to make human beings VERY protective of them. In fact not only do individuals become extremely protective over their beliefs - when challenged most will go on an all out offensive in their defense. Entire nations have been led to the brink of the abyss, desolation, even extinction in the name of them! However, a word to the wise - if you argue for, and vigorously defend your limitations then they are exclusively yours. Whatever you believe stops you from experiencing life as it really is, or really could be; in fact the tighter that we hold onto certain beliefs the more our mortal coil will be. So, another question…*what do you believe?*

Just one of my personal beliefs is that in many ways beliefs are at times akin to the death of intelligence, so I have a lot of opinions, but no beliefs.

That said belief in any cure amounts to at least half of the healing process…so don't be like me and stop believing.

Have a period of reflection on all of this…either now later or whenever…but *please do so…*

Infinity

Without letting the cat in the hat out of the bag we will return to the concept of death…*later*. However in the meantime do not, not *be positive about life and its endless wave of possibilities.* When the ˙ʳs of mice and men begin to get on top of you, you are ˥ because the car needs new tyres, the central heating has again, work is getting too much, your supposed ˙ʳiend is ignoring your texts… or the kids have not swapped out the empty toilet paper roll with a new one, please don't remember to forget to remember that you are actually living on a lump of rock, floating in infinity.

Infinity Exercise;

I'd like you to find a pen and a piece of blank A4 paper.

Please take a few minutes and cover that piece of paper with as many pen dots as you can.

When you are finished there should literally be hundreds of dots. Each dot represents a solar system. Circle one individual dot please. That's where you live by the way.

Now look at that page, and imagine it as the size of your widescreen TV (I know you probably have one!), then your living room wall, then your living room, then your house, then your street. Now, that's pretty big and there will now be many, many millions of dots. Now expand that picture to the size of your town, then your county, then your country. Once you have that picture expand it to the size of your continent. There will now be many trillions upon trillions upon trillions upon trillions of dots; utterly and completely uncountable and unquantifiable.

Thanks for doing that. Hang in there we are getting to the point.

Now, expand that picture to the size of the Pacific Ocean, then the planet. Great, now expand it to the size of the solar system, then the cosmos. Now there will be many trillions of trillions of trillions of trillions of trillions of trillions of pen dots ad infinitum; utterly and completely mind boggling and completely uncountable – utterly beyond our comprehension.

Now, remember you circled only one, the one where you live.

…..and we are not at this point even beginning to make the tiniest scratch upon the surface of infinity. Not even 0.00000000000000000000001%

Perspective is indeed a wondrous thing.

We undoubtedly live in an incredibly vast and unfathomably complex universe...scientists tell us that it just randomly came into being...so they say.

So, in life, whatever is *possible for others* is *possible for you*. In fact, lets take it a step further... impossible is impossible; it's impossible for it to be any other way. If you can do something about your problems then there is no point worrying, if you can't then worry is of no use. *Change the toilet roll, call a plumber, book the car into the garage, realise that you are your own best friend...and take the rest of the day off.*

Hey ho, onwards and upwards towards...

The most powerful organism in the known universe

I am, therefore I think

...but it is when I stop thinking that I am.

In the beginning of your life *you were a single cell,* formed when your father's sperm fertilised your mother's egg; this spectacular event taking place in your mother's fallopian tube, a safe haven connected to, and bridging the *Ovary* and the *Uterus*...a tidy, muscular expansive nurturing place the approximate size of a pear. *Do you remember?* At this very point your blueprint was determined, a chromosome from your fathers sperm determining whether you were to be male (Y) or female (X). There then followed the wondrous natural development of you, the miraculous human being that you undoubtedly are. Amazingly, at approximately 40 days after the initial fertilisation of the egg the brain waves of a human embryo can be detected by an Electro-encephalogram (more commonly known as EEG) which measures brain activity via electronic waves or pulses, classified as *Hertz*. Because of this many experts believe that *this is the point* that *the human* foetus *acquires sentient* capacity. This is entirely theoretical, however let's run with it for now.

So, to cut to the chase - yes, *you've got it*…congratulations at the centre of your nervous system pulling all of the strings *you own your* own *brain*. You possess your own version of the most highly complex biological organism in the known universe.

We often don't think about thinking much, we just think. So let's think about it now…

The brain is in itself one of our great literal and existential mysteries; it has powers and capacities that are, even with our current (embryonic) levels of understanding completely and utterly staggering. This organism is similar to other mammalian brains – however the key difference that makes the difference being that it has a significantly more developed cerebral cortex. It is an incessant thought generating and processing machine with a seemingly limitless potential and capacity.

But, wait - Houston… we have a problem;

- *We all have a brain but it doesn't come with a user instruction manual - and unmanaged the most powerful living biological organism in the known universe can run rampant and create complete and utter bedlam.*

In the normal waking Beta state your brains trusty sidekick and agent provocateur, the Mind incessantly, perpetually generates thoughts. It never shuts the hell up unless *you actively* take measures to *bring it under your control* and *discipline it*.

Being proactive in doing so is *incredibly important* for one other principle reason.

I must inform you at this juncture that *your brain is* also *highly suggestible to* the immense power of *your imagination*. In fact it takes imaginings quite literally. This obviously has potentially massive positive connotations, but sadly, more often frequently manifests in the negative;

- *The brain cannot tell the difference between imagined reality and actual reality. You need to be <u>very</u> careful about the way that you think.*

Never underestimate the power of your thoughts – they are <u>everything</u>. Every action is the result of a thought. If *you* don't *apply* some *control and order to your thoughts* you will inevitably and undoubtedly end up with internal chaos ...which will undoubtedly and inevitably become external chaos. Be assured, Adolf Hitler's insane, paranoid genocidal murder of millions of innocents began with his insane, paranoid genocidal murderous thoughts;

- *All human suffering is caused by the painful thoughts that our mind creates; believing these painful thoughts causes pain and human suffering.*

Thus we are not scared of what we think we are scared of. We are scared of what we think. You should *know now* that *most* of this incessant cognitive *thought activity* is *not* kind to you or *supportive to human well-being.*

It constantly analyses, and relives the past, punishing us for what did or did not take place – causing fear, anger, regret, sadness, hurt, resentment, guilt …and thus suffering. *It also constantly scans our present circumstances,* interpreting, projecting, alert to any potential threats, whilst simultaneously seeking to understand why things are happening – thus applying perceived meaning to all we experience… causing dissatisfaction, fear, annoyance, insecurity, jealousy, sadness, hurt, resentment…and thus suffering. *It also constantly perceives the future* through a lens of fear; punishing and torturing us with what might or might not take place like the Sword of Damocles hanging over us – causing needless worry, fear, anxiety and stress…and thus torment.

Harry

She came to see me with a simple and common concern; she was terrified of arachnids.

Every time she saw one she would become almost uncontrollable, hysterical…shaking, sobbing, barely able to even breathe. Before curing her phobia for all time I decided upon a simple experiment.

In perfect safety I watched her carefully as I confessed that I had a large Tarantula going by the name of "Harry" as a pet in a glass case in my home.

I told her that I had accidently left the lid off, and that it was currently on one of the walls – but assured her all was well because it was quite placid; she began to shake, her breathing changed, her skin tonus altered, she gripped the edge of her chair…she became terrified of the thought of my crawling arachnid pet…

I had of course used subterfuge - there was no Tarantula, or any other type of spider for that matter in my home. I had invented Harry. It did however serve to prove the entire point…

*She was not in fact scared of crawling arachnids at all, she couldn't be...there were none present...she was just scared of the **thought** of them!*

And so, I wonder how else people apply fearful thoughts of what actually isn't there in their lives...

The vast majority of our thoughts are completely and utterly pointless and do not assist or allow us to *respond appropriately to any challenges* that we actually do encounter.

They actually reduce our resourcefulness because our human tendency is to Delete, Generalise and Distort what we perceive - thus often stoking the bonfire of our emotions and as such *impacting upon our physiology and behaviours.*

Indeed as a consequence the incessant thoughts usually make our life experiences seem ever more difficult and thus we feel ever more helpless – and life consequentially then seems like a perpetual struggle.

The need to silence the constant chatter and *take a break* is one of the primary reasons for alcoholism, drug addiction; eating disorders, phobias, mental health problems...and the real reason why so many people are constantly *trying* to distract themselves in this modern age of (non) enlightenment with mobile phones, tablets, Ipods, electronic devices, huge televisions (which actually exacerbate the problem!).

There is however good news. *Hurrah!* (*Sound of trumpets trumpeting!*) You can actually learn how to gain control of your internal incessant brain activity. In fact *I strongly recommend* in the strongest possible terms *that you learn to* now.

It is actually ridiculously simple, takes not more than 20 minutes a day and with discipline and practice can become habitual - resulting in a sense of clarity, focus, connectedness and internal peace. The ability to achieve this is so much simpler and closer than you could ever have imagined. How can this be achieved you may ask, and yet…the answer is simplicity in itself. There is no religious creed or dogma, complex jargon or necessary adherence to some new age vision quest. Remember the whole point is to *be free*.

Here's the simple secret

- *Still the mind and live in the present moment.*

This process operates on a very simple premise;

Quieten your mind > Gain control of how you think > Change the way you think > Change the way you feel > Change the way you behave > Change your reality

Where the mind leads the body will follow and where the body leads the mind will follow.

Ancient spiritual wisdom, particularly in the Far East has espoused this for literally thousands of years. Deep Meditation and in particular, Mindfulness have become ever more popular in recent times; both of which when practised properly can be effective, empowering and even life affirming. Be assured right here and now that the potential benefits of these disciplines cannot be overstated. They serve as the best way to *quieten your mind, clear impurities from the human Nervous System* and *Cellular Structure*, thus enabling us to *connect with that which is more*…the divine cosmos.

Now, the following exercise is not radically different from many other Mindfulness exercises that you may or may not encounter; it is therefore no better or worse. It just is. I would however prefer that you term this as *Mindlessness* - after all the whole point is to *downshift, quieten* and *empty your mind...so less is more!*

Remember...language is an important part of our cognitive filtering process.

Mind*ful*ness versus Mind*less*ness = *less is more*

To avoid being perceived as pedantic or contrary, I will simply call this process *Mind Guidance*.

The essence of this practice is to be completely in the moment; open and aware... in *Now* as opposed to becoming embroiled in the incessant activity and judgements of the mind. The mind is complex...and we have been listening to it for our entire life, but separating ourselves from the perpetual thoughts brings independence from suffering and pain because we are allowing ourselves to *detach from Time and have freedom.*

Remember, the mind has the tendency to regretfully relive a painful past and postulate about a presupposed fearful future. A state of *Mindlessness mitigates and* thus *nullifies this.*

Mind Guidance exercise;

Throughout our life there has been one constant – that of breath. It is the perpetual, constant, essential physiological function; it accompanies us from birth to death. For this reason alone we should become acutely aware of it...and why wouldn't we?

Making and taking the time to put only ten minutes aside twice each day to practice the following exercise is an investment in self and excellent way to begin to lay the foundations of the Mind Guidance discipline;

- *Sit in a position that is erect yet as comfortable as possible, spine straight*

- *Close your eyes, go inside and begin to relax*

- *Use your abdomen and chest take several deep breaths – allow your lungs to fill …then completely exhale all of the air from your lungs. Be aware of how it feels to purposefully breathe in this way.*

- *After these initial breaths simply find a natural rhythm, allow your breathing to be as shallow or as deep as you like.*

- *Now pay attention to the affects of this breathing, the experience of the air entering and leaving your body through either the nose or mouth….either way is fine. Notice the rise and fall of your shoulders and chest …the movement of your abdomen.*

- *Be fully aware of how it feels to breathe – and become acutely aware of the spaces in between as it cycles naturally…become aware of the silence that surrounds you.*

- *Thoughts will come and go as you do this, this is to be expected. Detach yourself from them, just allow them to come and go. If you become aware that you have become lost in a thought then all you have to do is simply let it go, like a helium balloon… watch it float away and return your focus upon your breathing and the spaces in between.*

- *The mind will generate thoughts, accept this. The process is actually about learning to be able to notice them without becoming embroiled. This is at the heart of achieving mental discipline and eventual mind guidance. Thoughts will come; just observe them from a detached position and then simply return your focus to your breathing and the space in between.*

- *Continue for as long as you wish then gently return to full awareness by opening your eyes and reorienting yourself to your surroundings.*

- *Notice how you feel.*

Practice mind guidance twice a day, for ten minutes and be prepared to experience an increased awareness, focus, connectedness, peacefulness and joy. Like any other sort of exercise or discipline it takes practice, however always never forget to remember that the repeated act of performing any method of improvement leads to repeated improvement because a person's unconscious mind effectively and unquestionably adopts patterns and habits! After all, it has no critical faculty. Do not be concerned with how to do it "right" or "wrong" – these are illusory.

We are born without restrictions, and like fear they are either learnt or imposed upon us. When practicing mind guidance, if *you become aware* that your attention has drifted off simply return your focus to the present moment, your breathing, your body and the space in between… there is nothing else to do, nowhere else to go, no other rules!

- *If you aren't living in the present moment you aren't living a peaceful life.*

We are dead then we are born, we breathe, we live, then we stop and are dead and we do not. Of all of our basic human needs air is the most essential and fundamental. Breath is life, life is breath.

Don't think on that awhile whilst *you breathe* some more H20, carbon dioxide and oxygen… *in and out…in and out…*

Death

Life can be quantified as *Ars Moriendi... the art of dying.*

Death is the phase of existence that then succeeds life and is perhaps in itself often viewed as the greatest mystery of all.

This depends of course upon your own personal beliefs or emotionally based opinions. As a result it is thus open to infinite interpretation; however I intend to expand on this and explore it just a little further a little later.

So, to summarise this chapter I want to leave you with a significant reframe to think over, chew upon...consider if you like;

I probably don't know you or know what you are going through in your life right now, but given that anxiety and fear are at the root of all of our actions you have, are or will undoubtedly be suffering from these to some extent, and this will have a pervasive impact upon your well being.

But *you* should *live well* and remember this - when you are going through these hardships, whether you are riding the crest of a wave, drowning in a sea of hopelessness, a king, a pauper, famous, invisible, rich, poor, beautiful, nondescript, healthy, ill, a soldier, a tailor, a candlestick maker, a tree house builder or a stickleback stalker...*it's all an illusion.*

...we are all dead anyway.

2 HAPPINESS

Happiness, everyone knows what it is, don't they?

Well, here's the thing, it should seem obvious…but it is not. In fact I guarantee that your assumptions of what happiness actually is are likely to be wrong. Psychiatrists have found that we are generally awful at perceiving our own levels of happiness and estimating as to what will or will not allow us to be happy. Perhaps the biggest problem with happiness is that *happiness is* often completely *misunderstood*. Happiness is in itself actually a nominalisation - that is, you cannot fill a wheelbarrow with happiness and push it home to add to your stockpile!

Now, this aside, there are a few important guidelines that enable us to be happier in our normal daily lives, and that is what this chapter is all about. In truth, *you* can *take action right now* to start *being happier*…thus *improving your* overall quality of *life*. I will outline these aforementioned guidelines to allow *you* to *be happier* in your normal daily *life*, and as *a bonus* I also promise to serve you a small slice of almost instant happiness …*later*.

But first…

The pursuit of happiness has in many ways become what seems to be an obsession of the modern age. I have lost count of the times that upon being asked what they really want someone has replied *"To be happy"*. Actually, this is a perfectly reasonable response; yet is rendered ostensible, even arbitrary as when questioned further as to what will bring about this stated outcome the client has been rendered completely at a loss as how to quantify what" *being happy"* is.

Now, it stands to reason that you cannot arrive at your stated destination unless you know where you are going …or just as importantly how to get there!

Consider this;

Would you wait at a random bus stop, jump on-board the first random bus to arrive …and then randomly hope it would randomly take you somewhere fulfilling?

Or;

Would you stand by an unknown river bank, without method jump aboard an unknown boat and set sail for destination unknown hoping that unknown would be where you would want to be?

…that said, you could always await the next random bus or unknown boat and roll the dice once again…

I would suggest that this would be a highly flawed strategy and unlikely to yield anything other than an unsatisfactory result, and there is a significant reason for this;

- *People who feel that they have no control over where they are actually going have very low levels of base level happiness regardless of the experiences that they encounter both on the journey and upon arrival at the eventual destination.*

…Yet so many people actually live out their lives lacking direction or control, hoping for the best, but willing to accept whatever their own concept of fate (whatever that is!) decides to serve up.

Here's the thing - people are usually likely to accept second best or something that is average, not particularly great…not particularly bad – just okay. People are generally risk averse. This is based upon fear. Fear is pervasive and at the root of all of our actions or inactions, thoughts and feelings. Fear rouses the inherent internal saboteur inside us all. Let me explain;

You see - you were here yesterday, and you survived…this is a highly significant message for the reptilian part of your brain, the deepest survivalist within, located inside the *Limbic System* at the deepest core of your brain; part of the realm of your *Unconscious Mind*. Its primary function is survival; it wants you to be here today, and tomorrow – therefore if what you did yesterday worked and you survived then it becomes a template for survival. Why change an acceptable formula? You will notice that I used the phrase *"Acceptable formula"* and not *"Winning formula"*. Of course, there is a difference. Human beings as a species are generally very lazy and like water and electricity will tend to follow the path of least resistance – therefore acceptable will often just do nicely, thanks very much.

Furthermore, as human beings we habitually form habits – *habits that can be extremely difficult to break*. A habit is a habit is a habit…good, bad indifferent. They are all formed within the Unconscious Mind with the very best of intentions for the good of the individual; these good intentions however frequently equate to a right thing for the wrong reason or the wrong thing for the right reason…or a wrongly right thing for a rightly wrong reason…if *that makes sense?*

This is why we can all too easily become trapped within a zone of comfort, a state of inertia, of safe blandness…an impasse invoked by fear of loss, fear of risk, fear of failure, fear of hardship, fear of embarrassment.

This is constraining and debilitating, as *it is often through loss, through the illusion of failure, through hardship that we actually grow and become better!*

Here is another question, and this time…*really consider your answer;*

Are *you open to feedback?*

You see, success is not a function of immediate results; it is an ongoing synthesis of ongoing feedback.

Most people like to be heard, but life as we have already discussed is about equilibrium…it's the natural order of all things. So, if you want to be heard you should be willing to park your egoism, your individualism…and utilise your ears and listen in equal measure. Sadly a lot of people waste the opportunity to do so during their interpersonal communications; if the truth be known they are too busy thinking about what they want to say next…

The Sprint

When I was 16 years old I was actively competing to gain entry to the school athletics team to compete in the 100 metre sprint at the county school championships. The only problem was that only the four fastest boys would make the cut…and my time placed me at number seven.

The top two boys were very gifted; the fastest being particularly so.

Number three and four were naturally fast but undisciplined…number five and six don't feature in this story again. On the other hand, I was quite fast but neither especially gifted nor disciplined. No matter how hard I tried (tried) I just couldn't seem to get faster…so I decided to approach things differently. I sought advice. I sought feedback; and furthermore, and even more importantly…I used my ears. Boy number four did not seek advice, and probably would not have utilised those ears particularly well if he had in any case. He didn't need to, he was naturally fast.

Coaching makes a difference.

I was told to work on my rhythm, my co-ordination, my breath control, my start, my consistency…my strength. I practised on a field – not a flat, lush surface…rather an uneven, bobbled, unmanaged, wild country field with long grass and holes everywhere. I lifted large rocks to build upper body power. I learnt new, improved habits and remembered to forget the old ones…

During the final trials I placed fourth and made the team. I represented my school at those county championships; in front of a grandstand complete with crowd…I finished second in my first heat and progressed…but placed third in the next heat following a close race. Only the top two of six progressed. I remember feeling like a failure.

It was only later on reflection that I realised the true lesson of this experience.

In my year at school there were approximately 80 boys. I made the top four. At the championships there were around two dozen schools represented. That equates to an average pool of around 1920 boys…and then I realised that I actually did well - I was in the top twenty out of the entire county.

I never won a medal, but I effectively lapped the other 1900 boys that never made it on that early summer's day!

It's all about changing the frame of reference…

Incidentally, the number one boy that year ran in the final and won with an unofficial time of 11.4 seconds- an amazing feat for a 16 year old considering the world record at that time was just slightly over one second faster (9.93 seconds). He was an especially talented athlete. I met him again recently, 33 years after the event and it's both reasonable and fair to say that if we now raced I would probably win.

I'm not boasting, it would be neither fast nor pretty, however;

Life is not a sprint…it's a marathon.

Genius, Talent, Intelligence

Everybody has innate, latent genius, talent, intelligence…whatever you want to call it. Intelligence and talent are expansive and diverse in the extreme. For example, I personally know one particular genius who is endowed with a massive IQ; he doesn't know how to get a girlfriend, use a saw or wire a plug properly! I also know a school drop out who is bombarded with female admirers and can turn a pile of old discarded junk into objects of sublime art without much effort. Often the hand, eye and a degree of charisma can easily solve a problem that sharp intellect has struggled with in futility!

In my varied life journey thus far I have encountered a small number of individuals with an insane level of personal genius, but some, due to their ego, their gift, have displayed an unwillingness to accept feedback …and have subsequently settled into their niche, comfortable at their own particular, comfortable plateau. Their genius holds them back.

Now, this is not unusual by any means; this resistance to change, to develop and grow is linked to something that is firmly hardwired into our neurology in what is commonly known in psychology as *Loss Aversion*. Research into this has found that on average the discomfort of losing something is up to four times greater than the happiness of having it.

Whoa, how about that! Losing something hurts four times more than the joy of having it. Who'd of thunk it!

This loss can include virtually anything from a widescreen television, sports car, luxury villa in the Canary Islands …to kudos, reputation, status (*illusory*) and self importance!

Hence;

- *The happiness of having something is significantly less than the discomfort of losing it.*

Loss aversion is much like *Risk aversion*; it seems to be so fundamental that, for the reasons discussed it appears to be either God given or evolutionarily programmed into us. The divine Creator, Mother Nature (*or whoever or whatever else you hold responsible in your own model of the world*) wanted it this way!

So to paraphrase, your God, not your God, the reverse of your God or not the reverse of not your God has programmed it into us;

Regardless of who, how or why *it's there…it just is!*

However I digress slightly, a particularly bad habit of mine (*get it?*). My principal question to you, and I would like you to *really consider this for a moment,* is;

How can you have more happiness?

Many people are looking for external factors to make them happy, significant others, possessions, status, money, fame, fortune, power…pleasure itself. Now, in an appropriate context none of these things are necessarily bad – however this reliance on external factors is usually disempowering. It can be classified as External Validation. Furthermore, this disempowerment is compounded by a very humanistic trait;

We often overate that which we do not have…and underestimate that which we do have! Therefore;

- *If you always want what you do not have, you will never have what you want!*

If you have to *try* to be happy you will rarely ever be happy. Linguistically speaking *"Trying"* is a verb that is closely associated with *failing*. After all I don't *try* to breath, *try* to blink or *try* to get out of my chair, open the door and walk through to the toilet when I feel the need…I *just do it*. Why try when *you can* simply take action… and therefore *gain control*.

Happiness is like all other emotions, it's not something that we can own or obtain (like that wheelbarrow full I mentioned earlier, *remember?*)…rather, *you inhabit* it! When you are in a rage of anger, slamming a door shut, cursing and swearing at whatever has pissed you off you are not in a state of self consciousness, thinking;

"Aha, it appears that I am now angry…or am I? Is this real anger, how could I have more of it? If I only I could gain greater anger".

You just *are* angry, you inhabit it…you *are* anger…until it passes, and is gone.

In the same way as a person in a temporary state of passion doesn't wonder if they are *really* feeling passion, or a person in a temporary state of excitement doesn't wonder if they are *really* feeling excitement, a person in the temporary state of happiness doesn't wonder if they are happy …they just are. This indicates that happiness is itself not something that can be achieved in isolation, but rather that *it is a side effect to ongoing subjective life experiences*. This gets confused A LOT nowadays in our materialistic, fast paced modern age of instant (mis)information. Happiness is often *marketed at you* on an unconscious level as a goal;

" *If you buy this you will be happy*" "*If you buy that you will be happier*".

Incredibly, I actually read an article recently espousing a peculiar diet that guarantees you to be happier; the implications of this are staggering…not;

"My beloved pet cat has just died, and I should feel grief…but because of this accursed happy diet I just can't shake off the damn happiness and feel sad!"

You cannot buy happiness and you cannot achieve happiness…*it just is*, and it usually just is once you have attained balance, order and control in other parts of your life.

Happiness versus Pleasure

So, is there a difference between happiness and pleasure? In a nutshell, yes, a big difference. I shall explain:

When most people think that they are seeking happiness they are in fact actually seeking pleasure; food, drink, cigarettes, drugs, cars, houses, popularity, love, a six pack...and as great as pleasure is, it is just not the same as happiness. Granted, it is closely aligned to happiness in a mutual relationship, but does not cause it.

Wait a minute, *this is crazy talk!!*

Well, actually...it's not. Let me go on; ask any Heroin addict how much happiness the pleasure of consuming drugs has brought them. Ask the forty stone morbidly obese sugar addict how much happiness the pleasure of consuming vast amounts of all of the wrong types of food has brought them. Ask the alcoholic how much happiness the pleasure of ingesting consistently harmful amounts of poisonous alcohol has brought them....ask the multi millionaire lottery winner how much happiness the initial pleasure of having all that money in the bank has made them! Contrary to popular belief there are actually reckoned to be a higher percentage of depressed millionaires than those considered poor.

I kid you not, look it up!

The truth is that *pleasure is* a *superficial* form of life satisfaction, and therefore the easiest form...*it's quick and easy.* We become all too easily fixated upon it; we numb and distract ourselves with it. It is perpetually marketed at us on an unconscious level; and to this end I'm sorry to break this to you but ....*your mind is for rent.* If you don't believe me take the following test; If you can link these three phrases with huge multi billionaire companies then *sorry, you've been infected;*

...*I'm lovin it!*

...*Have it your way!*

&

...Finger lickin good!

Why do I ...*now feel hungry*? Now that you have read that ...*you* ...might... *feel hungry* too. *Feeling hungry now* ...is fine if ...*you need to eat*... not so great if ...*you* ...don't ...*need to eat now*!

Apologies, I couldn't help it…re-read the previous paragraph and see if you can pick out the *subliminal* NLP skull duggery that has been deployed. *Tip – read only the italicised words in bold text as a stand alone sentence to… *really get it.*

Allow for a cynical yet honest digression for a moment, you need to *know the following.*

You see, in keeping with those pillars of society, otherwise known as politicians and the media, multi billion corporations know all too well the power of the unconscious mind and NLP & hypnotic language patterns. Would you be at all surprised if I was to tell you that many of said organisations actually actively cultivate devious strategies to formulate and engineer habit forming products for you, the dear consumer? And you do know what *habit forming* really means don't you? Well, allow me to cut to the chase – it actually means the *cultivation of compulsive addiction*. Think tobacco, booze, soft drinks, chocolate, fast food, materialism (make no mistake, one of the shallowest forms of addiction).

An example;

This puts me in mind of a well known US tobacco company that ran a TV advert many years ago; picture the scene - a handsome doctor in a white physician's jacket with a stethoscope round his neck, drawing upon a cigarette whilst asserting "*Mmmmmm, good healthy cigarettes!*"

Sounds ridiculous, even obscene now…but an entire generation literally bought it and paid the price. Of course, *their methods are* much more *covert* nowadays…

I can assure you the list could go on and on.

And yet *you* the public, *invite them into your homes*…it's constantly beamed into your living rooms on the good old *hypnobox*, oops sorry…I mean television. Concurrently *you are* at the same time *constantly being manipulated* to feel guilty about the percentage of our society that is clinically obese, clogging up hospital wards, in debt or overindulgent!

Well, hello! Damned if you do, damned if you don't. *More on this later!*

Anyway, back on track after another detour (*my bad habit, agh!!*) Pleasure is necessary, but never ever enough. And here is why;

- *Some ongoing research is consistently illustrating that people who focus their energy upon superficial and materialistic pleasures are actually ending up more anxious, emotionally unstable and generally unhappy.*

Oh dear…what a downer ☹

Positivity

Do you know someone who always appears to be happy and carefree regardless of their circumstances and life situation? Do you envy them, perhaps wish you could be just like them? Well, here is the crux;

There is a strong possibility that this is the most dysfunctional, screwed up person that you know.

In truth this is probably, to some degree a form of denial - and denial of negative emotions actually leads to a downward spiral of negative emotions and emotional dysfunction. In truth *it's okay to be angry, it's okay to be sad, it's okay to moan, it's okay to be only be okay*....you are a sentient universal being and, *news flash* - *you own, and MUST express a full range of emotions.*

Consider this;

Remember our previous discussion about God/evolution/whatever? Here is further perspective;

Survival of the fittest - only the most adaptable and robust of life forms right here on good old planet Earth survive the continual evolutionary and/or supreme being generated process of natural selection. If humans were always ecstatically happy Gods / Mother Nature's/Whatever's process of natural selection would soon *weed us out* because we would be all too easily satisfied, lack ambition, settle for limited resources and would not meet the requisite survival of the fittest criteria. On the flip side, if humans were morbidly depressed all the time we would be weeded out by the natural selection process because we would not have sufficient motivation to achieve anything because everything would seem pointless!

Anyway, I digress (*I'm bad for that by the way*).

We are constantly bombarded in this age of (*too much*) instant *information* by happy, smiling, perfect people on the television, movies, pop culture and glossy magazines. This is an alluring false veneer of positivity that hides an undercurrent of hollow emptiness and misdirection. *It is mass manipulation.*

By the way, for those who insist there is no such thing as hypnosis...you're right - all of those people sitting engrossed in their mobile phones are just pretending to be a *in a trance*...(whatever that is.)

Now...to the modern cult of celebrity, the famous infamous for being famous for their famously infamous fame;

- *The singer and actress Britney Spears epitomises this perfectly; the poster girl for a generation, an icon who appeared to have everything ...yet she slowly unwound in a very public way, becoming engulfed in a maelstrom of negativity, depression, mental health issues, broken marriages, personal problems, child custody drama and a very public hair shaving episode that shocked her followers....*

Or

- *George Michael, one of the worlds biggest selling artists who during the 80's had it all, the talent, the hits, the fame, the looks, the wealth, the adoration of millions – before descending into a nightmare of high profile and very public sexuality related relational problems* (think public toilet), *drug abuse, physical & mental health issues, relationship woes...and eventual lonely death which broke a million female hearts.*

And whilst I'm on the topic of loneliness I want you to ponder the following. George was a musical genius, loved and admired by millions - but didn't know this;

> *If you love who you are, you will never feel lonely with the person you are with when you are alone.*

Anyway...I could illustrate this point again and again using multiple examples of the same phenomenon; those with *"it all"* who, when the going gets tough sadly and dramatically veer off life's proverbial piste and head for the cliff face.

But, regardless of whom you are, if you live in the *real* world then *shit happens*, people will piss you off, let you down and life will almost never be fair. *Bad things will happen to you*...a lot! You will screw up; you will make mistakes (a vital part of the learning cycle). Negative emotions will arise…but *that's* actually *as it should be* and is *absolutely fine.*

As with all things in life there must be balance. I shall illustrate how negative emotions can be very useful and thus form an essential part of the roughage of life;

- *Sadness* – allows us to process and internalize loss

- *Anger* – allows us to protect our values and boundaries

- *Anxiety* – usually guarantees enough motivation to maximise performance

- *Guilt* – allows us to avoid, or indeed right wrongs

- *Shame* – allows us to avoid repetitive wrongdoing

Life is rarely what it should be – it begins, runs its course then ends…but *it's what we do about the things that happen to us that makes the difference.* If we accept that bad things will happen, manage to deal with them in an appropriate way and take responsibility then we retain *Control*, attain *Internal Validation* and add fuel to the hearth of our base level happiness…

- *Without negativity there can be no positivity. Negativity is an essential part of maintaining a stable base level of happiness in your life. There can be no good without bad. Negativity is an essential part of the roughage of life's varied diet.*

Self Help

There are some positive aspects of what is an extremely crowded self help industry, however its single biggest failing is that it is just that…an industry;

"I'm going to allow you to help yourself by selling you my latest gimmick, that will allow me to help myself to the money you are paying me to help you help your self with my gimmick!"

Oh yes, try saying that with a mouthful of false teeth whilst rubbing your tummy and patting your head!

Money turns the wheels of industry, and the wheels of the self help industry turn on the premise that everybody needs help to help themselves all the time

(thus purchasing their products and feeding the business).

That aside, in real terms nobody can achieve anything truly meaningful in isolation; we all need help sometimes. So despite there being positive aspects of the self help industry be very wary of certain others, like *"The secret of instantaneous wealth"* CD's;

The secret is that the author is selling the secret to lots of people who want to know the secret to make ever greater wealth *through* the non existent secret. It's no secret…*yet, moths and flames…*

Fair enough you may say, we all need to put bread on the table - which we do *(unless you are on a gluten free, protein only, fruit, vegetable and dairy free, vegan happiness diet!).* The cogs of industry will always continue to grind on regardless of good self help, bad self help and everything else in between.

Is positivity always positive? No, beware;

There are some people who subscribe to the *"lets all be positive all the time!"* ideology. A word to the wise…avoid these people like the Black Death, *they are deluded.*

It is a hollow pretence.

Happiness, as we now know, is <u>not</u> a perpetual, never ending permanent state of hip hop happy time happiness. The denial and appropriate expression of negative emotions is in real terms an unhealthy suppression of a vital part of being human and leads to imbalance.

There must be balance in all things; it's the natural order…

Gratitude and its implications

Having established that balance is a prerequisite of the human living experience, and that adversity, negative emotions and sadness are as integral a part of our lives as the equal and opposite of such…how then can we then lessen the experiential impact of this and smoothen the transition from *that* and *those* which are *negative* back to *this* and *these* which are *positive*?

…well, through the practice of *Gratitude*.

Allow me to expand on this;

As has been discussed earlier in the *Life* chapter we live in *Now* and now consists of this moment only…which all time actually is.

This moment is all that really matters as the painful past and a fearful future are merely reflections of painful thoughts that your mind will incessantly generate if left to its own devices. So, *you* may or may not *realise it* but in each moment, great, good, bad, painful, different or indifferent *there is always much to enjoy and celebrate*, no matter how seemingly insignificant or cursory; all you have to do is be able to adopt a different perspective and *notice*, validate, celebrate *and magnify the positive*!

- *In the midst of every adversity there are always positive opportunities*

By actively taking the time to practice feeling grateful for all of the good aspects of your present circumstances, no matter how tiny, you will begin to feel better. In fact the results may prove to be more profound than you may ever have thought possible!

The act of *Gratitude* is a powerful way of reframing any situation and manifesting hitherto unseen opportunities; this in turn offers the key to the safe which actually houses some irrepressible benefits to deep personal wellness. It's not always easy to do, but it's worthwhile …*make the effort to do so.*

So, instead of becoming embroiled in complaining, moaning, anger, frustration, loss, sadness et al focus upon, and feel good about all that you have instead!

Gratitude > Increases Self esteem > Increases Resilience > Increases Happiness > Increases Empathy > Increases Tolerance > Reduces Sadness > Reduces Depression > Reduces Anxiety > Reduces Fear > Reduces Aggression > Reduces conflict

---

Therefore, if *you* actively *take the time to focus on the good* during bad times, and *show appreciation for* the *others* in your life, your life events, situations and circumstances will noticeably improve. *You are blessed in many ways.*

Everybody is.

Gone in a Stroke

He happened to be the gentleman who knew the magic words. Tall, handsome, fit, well coordinated and strong he was blessed with a razor sharp, witty mind. He was incredibly charitable and giving. This giving

extended beyond his own to his others, his local community - which benefitted from his presence.

He was a people person, possessed social skills and as a result loved company.

He would always never walk past anyone without a friendly "Good Morning, how are you today?" … which I might add was not and remains not the norm for the West coast of Scotland! This would often result in a surprised surly look, a fixed stare as though he was invisible and mute, or a stuttering reply of "…Oh, eh, yes…eh good morning" as they rushed on by as they kept pace in the race of rodents.

None of that bothered him one iota, he just loved people and always sought the human connection. It mattered not in his model of the world if they chose to ignore him, chat for awhile or otherwise. He chose to choose to never let it hurt his feelings…

He suffered a serious stroke at a relatively young age and in one fell swoop his physiological fitness, strength and co-ordination were gone for all time. He was however blessed with a razor sharp witty mind and his cognitive fitness, strength and co-ordination were there for all time…and he still knew those magic words. Against doctors orders he survived for another fifteen years to welcome me and all but one of his grandchildren into this life. Most of his physical health had deserted him, but he enjoyed a healthy life by noticing the small things that made a difference and being grateful for the glory of life. He knew the magic words and used them a lot…especially to those who obliged. He was especially grateful for those who were especially grateful for him… and sooner, later or whenever he did let them know.

I recall he would usually sit outside in his small front garden with a cup of tea and his faithful companion gratefully enjoying the little, good things in his life and would never watch anyone walk past without a friendly "Good morning, how are you today?"

He was my best friend and lowering him to the ground was the saddest of my sad times. I do however remain eternally grateful for him…

Thank you god for him, thank god for him the wind beneath our wings.

By focusing on the good we gain better control of our thoughts and this will positively impact upon our feelings, our relationships with ourselves, our relationships with others and our relationship with, well…everything! *You* may find yourself *becoming more optimistic, less stressed,* less concerned with materialism and *less envious of others*…your psychological health will consequentially improve. Remember, where the mind leads the body will follow… thus your physical health will then respond and react by actually reducing the toxic chemicals within the cellular structure of your very own body. More on this….*later!*

So, *take just two minutes* at the beginning and end of each day to just stop and *really consider all of the things that you have to be truly thankful for*. When was the last time that you openly expressed your gratitude to the people in your life who mean so much to you? When was the last time that you took the time to notice and validate all of the things that you are lucky to be able to experience in your life? I strongly suggest you *do so* because the act of expressing this will increase your own personal happiness in ways that may just surprise you.

Count your blessings and be grateful!

Your Ideal Self

Anyway, thanks for hanging in there…you are doing really well. We are getting to the business end of things. Please read on;

I mentioned *External Validation* earlier; you know, when you allow your sense of base level happiness to be decreed by the judgment of others; by material possessions, by status, rank and class (*particular favourites of the deluded*), power (*another delusion*), living up to those high profile celebs. You've all seen them - happy adverts (designed by unhappy people to utilise unhappy people to mass market an unattainable happiness for the masses to aspire to, thus becoming unhappy too).

Fame, a six pack, an AUDI convertible, perfect teeth, wonderful hair (but hey, *you're worth it!*) blah, blah and blah ad infinitum.

The antidote to this male bovine excreta (*bullshit to you and I*) is *Internal Validation*. This can be attained through proactively *taking the responsibility* to take *action* as you work towards your *ideal self*;

For example;

- *Running a marathon is painful, unpleasant and requires sacrifice and dedication; by the way it is also guaranteed to endow you with more happiness than eating a box of Cadbury crème eggs, or a quarter pounder with cheese and large fries followed by a cinnamon donut and milk shake every day...just saying!*

Now, setting this type of goal as you move towards your ideal self requires focus upon a particularly high outcome, and there is the real possibility of *failure* (*WOOOO...be afraid, be very afraid!*) yet success likely to be one of the *truly meaningful* moments of your life regardless. The pain, struggle, anger, sacrifice and exhaustion are posthumously forgotten when recalled long after the actual event. This is because these types of activities allow us to move closer towards being the best that we can be...our *ideal self!*

This experiential state of taking action, of *becoming more* is rich in happiness. Achieving goals, taking responsibility and *gaining control* allow us to be happier. You need to remember the things that you enjoy, and do them.

The artist must paint, the writer must write, the actor must act, the musician must make music, the carpenter must saw, the electrician must wire, the genius must prove their genius by doing very well at Mensa IQ tests… to ever truly be at peace with themselves.

Incidentally, anyone who actually seriously believes that by doing awfully well at a Mensa IQ test proves their high level of superior intelligence *has* in reality *failed* the real test…*think about it*. But I digress (*again…dammit!*)

Of course, running a marathon is an extreme example; as always, it is all about context. The legendary hypnotherapist and psychotherapist Milton H, Erickson, one of his generations outstanding (*and at the time often ignored and vilified*) geniuses, crippled since his teenage years by polio, once smiled and said with a twinkle in his eye;

"*I win Olympic championships out of my wheelchair everyday!*"

So, what exactly did he mean?

Well, Milton H. Erickson's mother was told by a doctor that her son would not live past 17 years of age. Milton decided not to take that piece of medical advice, struggled out of bed each day …and made his indelible mark upon the world until the age of 78.

He ended up 61 years in credit.

The attainment of this simple goal each day, to get out of bed, is actually a powerful reframe. Imagine who you actually want to be, and then actively move towards it. *Take action*. Do something to *become more*. If what you are doing isn't working then do something else, anything else. Push beyond any boundaries imposed upon you and mark out your own!

If you do take this action I guarantee that you will *change* the way you think, which will *change* the way you feel which will *change* the way you behave... and you will *be inspired;*

Step by step

Following a particularly debilitating back injury several years ago, and different misdiagnosis from not one, not two but three general medical practitioners (who all disagreed with each other) and two physiotherapists who were unable to agree, a renowned osteopath examined me.

He informed me that due to the nature of my pelvic, sciatic and lumbar disc damage things would never quite be the same again, namely I could no longer run and should consider changing my profession. At the time I could barely even walk... and as you can imagine this advice took me aback as up until this point I had been running at least 30 kilometres per week.

I needed to process this advice, so I walked for ten minutes each day for a week and thought about it, my leg hurt from sciatic pain but no answer was apparent... so I then walked for twenty minutes a day for another week and thought more of it...my leg still hurt, yet I still needed to reflect on this life changing advice. So I walked for 30 minutes each day for a week and gave it more thought. More reflection was required so I decided to remember to forget my leg pain for awhile and determined to run a mile each day to give it more thought...it was painful, but allowed quality thinking time...

Within six months of unconscious cortical remapping I was running three miles a day as I continued to struggle as to how I would deal with being unable to run anymore. What was I to do, how would I cope? Today, several years later I am still considering this conundrum as I run, yet I am at a loss as to how to deal with how not being able to run will impact upon me.

I plan to run some more until the answer presents itself...

In *taking action* this way I set simple, achievable and scalable goals; and as a result I never strayed too far from my base level happiness. I feel this is a good representation of the *psychological immune system* at work; it always stokes the hunger for more. Sooner or later, regardless of life events we all tend to return to our personal *base level happiness*.

Think about this *now, soon, or later...but give it some thought.*

Improving personal happiness

I have mentioned *Base level Happiness* a few times already, but what does it mean? Well, I equate it to your natural state of happiness; some people have quite a high level of it, others less so...it's individualistic.

Everyone has a different level and it can be affected by life events, but hey...we are after all bespoke and open to influence! Surprisingly, research has showed that we actually inherit at least 50% of our level of *Base level Happiness* during our formative childhood development from parents, siblings, environmentalism etc. The good news is that we can raise our level of *Base Level Happiness* depending on how we interact with, and react to or experiential existence; after all we still have approximately 50% of our *BLH* to play around with and maximise.

How so? Again, by having a sense of *direction, purpose,* of *control,* of *taking action* and following one step with another ...and yet another; by allowing ourselves to express our emotions appropriately but remain predominantly positive whilst striving for more...these are the essential ingredients to bolstering our *Base Level Happiness*.

So, without further ado to my first promise at the beginning of this text to outline the important guidelines to living a happier life;

- Guideline one - *Take responsibility for everything that happens in your life.*

Life is rarely what you or others think it should be; shit will happen to you...it's what you do about it that makes the difference. *The truth about real power is that it can never EVER be taken*; you can only acquiesce and give your personal allowance away;

Joan of Arc

Amid the flames and black smoke Joan of Arc, tied to her perch laughed aloud at her audience and continually yelled "Do you think that I am afraid? – this is what I was born to do!" Afterwards her executioners dug her charred body from the coals and burnt it again; a process they repeated one further time...

Joan may have been burnt alive at the stake, and her remains burnt twice more for good measure – but she decided to hold onto her power... and preferred that it burn and become dust rather than being gifted to her detractors for their pleasure...

Joan of Arc was as good as her word and she was not afraid – she burnt, not once, not twice...but three times, and her power still prevails.

...you only have that which you can hold!

Think about that last vignette for a moment...*really think about it.*

Don't ask *"why did this happen to me?"* and waste your time seeking meaning where there is none...ask *"What can I do about it?"* instead. After all one of the greatest human freedoms is that of being able to choose one's attitude to whatever is playing out...in this way *you always retain an element of control.*

If *you* need feedback and guidance then *seek* wise *counsel* ...*listen,* and *improve.*

- Guideline Two – *Have courage, regardless of your/others fear.*

You will form countless habits in your lifetime by virtue of your *Unconscious* minds unquestioning willingness to serve you. Why not form some really good ones – like *bravery.*

The paradox of being a member of humanity is that the survivalist *Reptilian* aspect of your brain will almost constantly hold you back due to *Risk/Loss aversion* through *Fear.* This is the *Fight, Flight, Freeze* response programmed into you by God, Evolution, Mother Nature, the universe...or whatever else floats your boat. It just **is**, regardless of whom, why, what and whatever...*remember?*

The lesser the courage > The lesser the control > The lesser the control > The lesser the action > The lesser the action > The lesser the gain.

Have courage.

- Guideline Three – *set realistic, achievable goals;*

It's probably best not to decide to lose weight by following the herd mentality and announcing to the world from the rooftops, or the modern day equivalent, Facebook and Twitter;

"I really mean business this time folks. Get outta my way - I am going to go to the gym four times a day, every day, whip myself with a riding crop, only eat grass and carrots, drink raw eggs and lose three stones this month...!"

This will be likely to result in only one outcome ... social embarrassment and copious indulgence by way of Ice Cream, cheesy Doritos and Prosecco to soothe the pain of failure...just saying!

Be stoical and decide to build Rome brick by brick in a timely, patient and civilised manner. If you need to crawl before you walk, before you run...then do so...and enjoy the journey.

- Guideline Four – *Accept only those judgements you make of yourself.*

If that puts you into a minority of one...and that is your truth, then so be it. *Internal Validation* is good; through it you automatically generate self reliance, self-respect and cultivate your own quiet garden of *personal power*. It is yours and it cannot be taken - only you can relinquish it. Through *Internal Validation* you follow your own moral compass, live by your own code of ethics and meet your own standards regardless of what others say, think or do.

External Validation is, well...often not so good. It has its place, but *constant* reliance on it amounts to acquiescence. It is all about appearance, seeking attention, getting approval from others, giving weight and credence to their judgements of you. It is a *hollow pretence*. Sadly, it is also very common in the western world, manifesting in materialism and celebrity culture. Through *External Validation* you crave the fast car, status, dream house, six pack, and perfect hair *(but hey...you're worth it!)*...and you relinquish much of your power in the process.

Be true to yourself.

- Guideline Five – *think about the bigger picture.*

Sometimes it is actually quite tricky to differentiate between *Internal Validation* (hooray, loud applause, fanfare, smiling children and cute puppies wagging their tails!) and *External Validation* (boo, hiss, rotten tomatoes, angry Rottweiler's straining at the leash…get off the stage!).

As Human beings we will always do what we think is the right thing to do at any point in time. You wouldn't decide *"This is really stupid…okay let's do it!"*…but sometimes, when wandering in the deep, dark woods, and the tree's are nowhere to be seen we just need to hit the pause button and get some objectivity. Despite noble intentions it is healthy to practice self awareness by gauging the course you are on and BE HONEST enough to decide if it really the right thing for the right reasons. Many don't take the time or are simply unwilling;

This is very hard for most of us because it requires objectivity, honesty, effort and a higher level of thinking.

Cultivating a greater perspective beyond ourselves is healthy and contributes to our *Base Level Happiness*. This can be cultivated through meditation, coaching and therapy, helping others (in any variety of ways), being charitable, being kind and seeing beyond our own superficial desires…doing the simple things well.

Happy times

And that's it for now folks; the end of this particular chapter. I would just like to say on behalf of…

"…wait, wait – you promised us a slice of instant happiness at the beginning and I have sat through all of this patiently waiting, where is it?!?!?!?!?"

Whoooooops, sorry about that… I forgot fully to not forget fully to remember to not forget to remember to tell you that!

To be honest I completely forgot about my amnesia!

Apologies, but what can I say; my badinage is of a poor quality …but give me a break. For the cheapskate price of this book what do you expect?

Okay fellow occupant of planet Earth, read on;

A slice of happiness exercise

You have learnt many things and have then forgotten that you know much. It's okay, that's how it's actually meant to be.

Sit up, spine straight, with your head held high, if you are standing then stand tall and erect…posture is very important, and let's begin….

Just relax while you now remember something that you know but had forgotten…

You will have experienced much happiness in your life at some point. Remember a <u>really</u> happy event in your life, something that happened to *you that was exceptionally positive and joyful; something wonderful.*

Once you have it explore the memory, see it through your younger self's eyes…notice people who were there at that time, the feelings you felt.

Notice the sounds, smells…remember how good it was….remember the wonderful atmosphere…savour it!

Now crank up the image, make it bigger, brighter, more colourful…bring it really close and immerse yourself in it.

As you make the adjustments to the visualisation notice any changes in the way you feel now…increase the emotional connection. Get back in touch with those great feelings.

Play the sounds, make them louder, and improve the clarity & tone. If there are others there then notice the happiness of those around you…the love you felt for them...how loved and special you felt…

Experiment with the experience and do whatever you need to do to make it as wonderful as possible!

Savour it for as long as you like, take your time. Only as soon as you are ready read on…

How was that experience? How good did it feel? I know that *you just felt happiness.* Unbeknown to you a complex process has actually just occurred;

It starts with a thought. Everything does.

Here is why that felt good. *Neuropeptides* are protein based molecules that are used by neurons to communicate with each other in order to influence the brain. They are classified as one of a group of *neurotransmitters* and were originally only thought to exclusively be found in the brain. However following the discovery that they are actually intrinsic throughout the cellular structure of the entire immune system we can actually determine now that the immune system is not separate from, or even working in conjunction with the brain…it is in actual fact an extension of it!

So, when you think happy thoughts your brain actually *releases feel good Neurotransmitters* (or hormones/chemicals if you like)…notably;

- *Serotonin, Dopamine and Oxytocin…*

These *Neurotransmitters* travel through your nervous system. They then spread through the *Cellular Structure* of your body, converting from chemical structure to electronic pulse, to bridge *Synaptic Gaps*, and then back many thousands of time in many thousands of a second; it's a naturalistic, all over feel good factor!

Incidentally, this is the same *Serotonin* and *Dopamine* that many prescription anti-depressants either simulate or contain. Conversely, when you think negative thoughts the same process occurs, except this time the *Neurotransmitters* that are principally released are;

- *Cortisol, Norepinephrine and Adrenaline*

These stimulate a heightened, protective, preventative reaction & reactionary response within our Cellular Structure.

This is no fanciful malleable fictional scientific theoretical notion – this is empirical Scientific Fact (*It is!*); every time you change your state of consciousness with thoughts, you literally change your *Neurochemistry*.

- *Anti-depressants - The lack of happy thinking creates a shortfall in naturally generated feel good chemicals; this shortfall is supplemented by what is in essence a prescribed chemical supplement.*

So, remember, as human beings we habitually form habits, good, bad or indifferent. It's the way we are wired deep within the *Limbic System* of our brain…part of the realm of the *Unconscious Mind*.

Live life, *accept the high and lows*, express your full range of emotions appropriately, set achievable *goals* and take realistic *action* to work towards them. Embrace *Internal Validation, be stoical* and retain *control*.

Habitually think happy thoughts, be optimistic more often and you will see an increase in your *Happiness* as a result.

Is that something you might be interested in…now?

3 PEOPLE

I'm a derivative of people, a person…and, that *being* said I'm *happy being me. You* should *do likewise.*

One thing that has struck me thus far during my current tenure upon this particular planet is that it is full of people…there are lots and *lots of people all over the place*! I have further noticed that people are primarily comprised of either men or women; apparently men originate from Mars and women originate from Venus…but as of yet I have been unable to uncover any notable evidence that can verify this! Another thing that I have noticed is that *people* generally *all want the same fundamental things,* you know…to *be safe, fed, comfortable, protected, validated, important, loved, admired, fulfilled* etc.

Now, an aphorism is that everyone is different; each man and woman is bespoke, that is highly individualistic. I don't know you, I don't know what you are not, are or otherwise going through…the only thing that I know is that I am an expert on being me, I am good at it and nobody does it better. I do however consequentially think *each person is* somewhat of *a people puzzle*…not only to me and to other people, but typically unto themselves.

- *I guarantee that you are a mystery unto yourself to a greater or lesser degree. So…what secrets are you keeping from yourself?*

This often manifests as a general lack of self awareness of who one is, what one is; why one is the way one is, does what one does, how one interprets ones experiences and how one can *take action to* cultivate an attitude of *becoming something better*.

So…let's explore this.

It seems to me that as each person is a microcosm of the macrocosm they therefore contain a deeply personal inner cosmos; and as such it is impossible to simplify and place any person into a nice neat little box of classification - after all if it was possible each person would require their own unique neat little box, and that would literally be billions of boxes…and that wouldn't work! Reality is a complex version of reality folks, regardless of how much you simplify your own!

This makes me *very curious*, and *you* should *be* too, because if you are not *curious* then you are literally not *exploring yourself*, others or your environment…the lump of moist spherical rock which is gently floating in infinity which you just so happen to reside upon.

Curiosity is a very positive state of arousal, a desire to know and learn. *As a child you were* infinitely *curious* about yourself, your environment and what else was out there. Do *you remember*? Others and other things other than other things were another thing to be infinitely curious about…you were unconditionally exploratory in an excitable way - but then you became an adult and learned not to be;

The Village

In the small country village where I was raised we were surrounded by the country...from the rugged hills to the woods, fields, rivers, tunnels and deep waters, as a child... we explored it all. We had free access to alien planets, spaceships, wild Western forts; football stadiums...during the summer our bicycles transformed into powerful futuristic motorcycles and our inflated bus tyre inner tubes became Native American canoes; during the winters our sledges became arctic skidoos and our bin liners became sledges. We had glorious fun terrifying ourselves of the witches, ghosts, night stalkers and werewolves that stalked our village during the hours of darkness. There was always an exciting adventure to be had, new territory to pioneer.

It was our gilded stage and we were the players, performers and portrayers. At times it was heaven.

Then one by one we grew up, and one by one we escaped...

When we *find a way of doing things* and being, we tend to establish this as the way, remember...human beings are habitually habitual by virtue of the fact that the limbic system of our brain always seeks patterns, to draw parallels. However;

- *There are always many ways to do anything. The enlightened say that no way is the way...it is just a way.*

A thought; when you wake up each day and get dressed...what trouser leg do you put on first? Furthermore, once you are dressed which shoe do you put on first? Okay, now....*why is it that you do that?*

*There is a reason, there must be…*but you probably are not even consciously aware that *you are doing the same thing every day! However here's the thing…your unconscious mind knows, and it knows why.* And it does.

Have *you* considered having a go at doing things another way and thus *becoming adaptable*? After all, if *you can adapt you* are infinitely *more adaptable'* and thus *resourceful*.

As a trainer I was at various points coined as a subject matter expert in my field – a term that I very much dislike. Why? Well, to me an expert is someone who has found a very particular and effective way of understanding, comprehending and doing something…therefore their relationship to their area of expertise is in actual fact very focused …and thus often very narrow. Whenever I found a particularly effective way of doing something I would then seek another way that worked really well, and then another and so on so forth. As we have already discussed by changing our way of thinking we will be able to change that which we are thinking about. Many "experts" actually tend not to do so.

The Same way

As a musician a few commentators made a few comments about the way that I didn't play the songs in the exact same way as the original or even as other non original originals;

To this I simply replied "I play the songs the way they are meant to be played at that time, not the way that they are, were or will be played by me or anyone else!"

In fairness I hardly ever played the same song the same way twice three or four times on the same day or days.

It keeps things interesting...

Consider this; only the most efficient, fit and adaptable of organisms survive right here on the good old planet Earth – and to *adapt* you need to *be curious*. Fear is the opposite and reverse of curiosity and it often literally prevents us from the exploration of *what could be* instead of what is. As such a lack of curiosity will be likely to restrain a person within the confines of the sad, bland, boring, saggy old grey comfort zone.

This can obviously in most circumstances be *un problema!* There is however an antidote to this and as always it is very simple;

- *Two of life's freely and readily available essential constants to the individual are those of Change and Choice.*

Yes indeed, good old *Change* and *Choice* are immensely powerful resources that, when wielded with clarity, direction and confidence allow for the actualisation of human freewill... and for the individual to literally grasp control of ones own destiny. For example, change often leads to insight more often than insight leads to change.

Now, how magical is that?

Change, Choice, Debt, News... Psychopaths & Sociopaths

You always have choices available...always. You can always choose change...always.

Many people wish something would happen; many want

something to happen, many people mourn that something hasn't happened ...others *make something happen!* So - are you at cause or effect?

Life is nothing more than a myriad of small decisions fed by change and choice. Think about it, *Change* and *Choice* offer one control of ones destiny, but, and it's a BIG but, many people would rather avoid change at all costs and prefer to hand the reins of their speeding chariot to *A-N-other*, which *A-N-other* incidentally particularly loves and will of course often seek to take maximum gain from. In this way the "elite" and the "courageous" win the non existential but quite literal human race of rodents, commonly otherwise known as *Survival of Fittest*. Oh, and by the by, *courage* does not equate to *fearless* – courage is in fact the ability to push beyond the fear that is undoubtedly being experienced by the brave.

The courageous *choose to "suck it up" overcome fear* and are *open to change*, thus *becoming adaptable, flexible, better*...and thus end up *"winning"*.

Now, *tangent alert*...don't get me wrong, at least some of these people register on the sliding continuum scale of *Psychopathy* and *Sociopathy* and as such are much less bound by fear and *risk aversion*, which impedes a general public comprised mainly of *neurotics*. In many ways those that make up the willing minority accept and *embrace responsibility* with what is a pervasive reliance upon an unwilling majority who won't, don't and subsequently believe they *cant*...often to advance their own fundamental agendas and selfish gain.

- Can't - *a linguistical contruction* = Can + Not. *Can't is a presupposition of inability, but is in actual fact that act of being able (Can) to not do something. When you assert "I can't" you are saying "I can, but am not"*.

The aforementioned psychopathic and sociopathic personality types would usually laugh internally at the naïve, neurotic concept of *can't*, as they simply *do or do not until they can do… then they do*.

- Don't – *another linguistical contraction* = Do + Not. *Don't is often used as a presupposition of disability, but is in fact the act of not doing as opposed to not being able to do... Same principal as can't…think about it!*

Now, don't misunderstand me – Psychopaths and Sociopaths are flawed, sometimes even dangerous…but are generally misunderstood. As a result I think you should really understand what I am about to clarify;

Psychopaths have <u>no</u> empathy whatsoever for human beings. You may have noted that I did not say other human beings - this because they are in many ways fundamentally quite inhuman. They have no conscience, a very high threshold for risk and fear and own a complete sense of superiority and entitlement that is <u>absolute</u>. They are exceptionally manipulative, convincing and incredibly skilful at mimicking and faking emotional connection with others. *Psychopaths have wiring loose in their heads.* There is a general perception that all Psychopaths are serial killers and mass murderers, and in the most extreme cases *this can be true*; however on the sliding scale these types are very, very rare as they grade at a 10/10…more commonly they can range from 1 – 9. It is estimated that approximately <u>1/16th</u> of human society have psychopathic or sociopathic tendencies to some degree…*did you realise that?* Sociopaths share much of the same traits; however the key difference is that they DO have some level of conscience.

Both types view themselves as Tigers and the rest of the population as Antelope and ceaselessly seek power and privilege.

Many low and mid level Psychopaths and Sociopaths are literally drawn to areas of war and conflict; for just one example think Middle East.

Oh yes...

It takes a special type of person to decapitate someone who is bound and helpless with a 6" blade, or place another human being into a cage before pouring petrol over them and setting them alight whilst being filmed as part of a propaganda campaign. And, let's make no mistake and be clear on this - fighter pilots launching devastating reigns of high powered, devastating explosives upon potential areas of helpless civil population from a lofty, disassociated position differ only in that they don't get blood on their hands like the "Baddies."

What is right and what is wrong? Do two wrongs make a right? It's just not that simple. Context and subjection defines each.

All war, violence, vengeance and conflict is a vicious circle, eternally suffered by the masses (those Antelope who *"can't"*) and enjoyed by the few (the Tigers who *"do"* or if unable to *"do"* wait until they *"can"*)...however, in the end the meek actually always inherit the Earth regardless. For example, through *passive non-resistance* the meek always *triumph*. Ghandi defeated the British, the most powerful military empire of the modern age this way. The Dalai Lama also continues to do so in exile; his poor, tiny Tibetan homeland occupied by one of the numerically mightiest military regimes of the modern age.

The fact is, in real terms such oppressive regimes are made to look uncouth by non aggressive inactions of passive resistance. How you may ask? Well, for a start you *turn the actions of others against them simply by amplifying your own weakness*... thus highlighting their bankrupt morality, decisions and actions. This simple reframe has been known to neutralise the strongest foe. Now, don't get me wrong, this is not how it works in the animal kingdom where the law of survival of the fittest prevails – but, hey….people, we are people…*remember?*

- *Hate never defeats hate, darkness never overwhelms darkness – only love does.*

A word to the wise – as difficult as it undoubtedly is (I know, I learnt the hard way) always do your best to avoid the destructive base feelings of anger, hate, revenge, resentment, jealousy et al to others. It is akin to drinking a cup of poison and expecting the other person to die!

You and you alone are the one that will suffer.

Anyway, back on track, war zones aside many other low level variants of Psychopaths and sociopaths simply just stay at home and create small scale war, havoc and conflict. This usually manifests in "normal" environments; their overwhelming sense of frustration at not having that which they "deserve" being utilised to perpetrate petty disharmony. Workplaces, social interactions and social media are particular favourites. *Is there someone in your office or place of work like this?* Higher level variants are often to be found in the higher echelons of banking, the stock market, government office, politics…*and much higher.* Oh yes!

So, a question or two;

Do you know anyone that could be graded on the *Psychopathic* or *Sociopathic* scale…say a 1/10 or a 3/10 or so? Could you even place yourself on the scale?

Have an honest think about that…the basic understanding of this is perhaps a powerful reframe for you. Beware (*Be + Wary = Beware*) psychopaths and to a slightly lesser degree sociopaths – they can seriously spoil your day and urinate upon your chips. If you are one to some extent then what (if anything) are you going to do to mitigate for this unpleasant trait of yours?

Whoa, that was a tad serious! Hey, forewarned is forearmed. It's just the way I roll sometimes. A bitter truth is always better than a sugary sweet deception.

Protect yourself...

Now changing tack slightly, the aforementioned aside have *you* ever considered that everything that any person has ever done since birth has been done so because they actually want something? As a baby you cried for milk and attention, and as you developed you learnt more subtle or elaborate ways to influence others to *get what you want*;

- *Every interaction is a manipulation.*

All human action is born of the desire for a purpose of personal attainment. If care is not taken then the virus of greed feeds from the desire for attainment like a leech. Second only to our primary urge and drive to procreate as outlined in the "Life" chapter is our sense of *Ego, Importance* and *Pride*; often however these are only roused as a reactionary response and are predominantly underused in a catalytic way for developmental growth. Tread carefully my friends, quite often *Ego, Importance and Pride come before a stumble ...and tumble!*

Anyway, when it boils down to *Choice*, well... many people avert themselves from it because they don't like to take responsibility and *Choose*. I sincerely empathise with *those* whose *current life circumstances* limit their present choices to unpleasant ones – however I would stress this; *if the things in your life continually aren't working do something else.* In fact do anything else.

Fear of choice is based upon fear of responsibility. How crazy is that! Life is actually a series of small decisions, and *Choice is* in actuality *great* because you can't choose unless you have choice. So...*how much choice is too much choice for you?*

Know that….you cannot reap what you have not sown.

If you have choice *you have options*…and if *you have options you are* more *resourceful. You* can never *be* too *resourceful*. The universal constant of change decrees that all things end and that all people change….but the river of life flows on regardless. You can either go with the flow or struggle upstream. When it boils down to *making a Change,* it's all about being willing to grasp the nettle and *accept responsibility for your own life.*

- ***Responsibility = Response + Ability.*** *Responsibility is the ability to be proactive by accepting their circumstance and then responding in an appropriate way.*

Massive changes are not required to implement massive change – after all when steering a ship it only takes a small, persistent deviation of only one degree to ultimately result in a very significant alteration over the course of the passage.

Small change + Small change + Small change + Small change + Small change + Small change = **BIG CHANGE**

So whilst *me and I* and *each and both of you* are on the subject, in a moment I would like you to really think on the following…if *that is okay with you;*

- *How big is your goldfish bowl or pond? What's holding you back in your life and what small choices are available for you to make small changes to affect an eventual BIG change? Are you willing to take responsibility for these?*

The Chosen Life

He spoke to me after hearing about me, about the problems of his life. He was living an emotionally and thus physically painful life...had money troubles because he had chosen to spend too much of it on not enough to feel better... which he didn't, suffered depression, anxiety, stress and was plagued by worry, uncertainty... fear.

It became apparent to me that he had decided to become buried in an intricate web of limiting beliefs, self imposed restrictions and low self confidence.

He had trusted others to assume control of his life and they had mostly been somewhat untrustworthy.

The Doctor had chosen to allow him to change by giving him lots of tablets.... He had chosen to reach rock bottom and with nobody else to assume control and change his destiny had decided to choose God to assume responsibility.

God however doesn't pay the bills and in fairness donated the resource of freewill long ago;

If you give someone a fish you feed them for one day – if you give them a rod, some line, a hook, an infinite source of maggots and a prime riverside spot they can apply for a fishing permit and feed themselves for the rest of their lives!

Anyway, I couldn't help but notice that he had already decided not to change...and as such was not open to suggestion.

At one point he said "I watch painful things on television that cause me great pain - the more and more I watch painful things on the television the more and more pain I feel." He asked "What can I do?" – to which I replied..."Well, what would happen if you turned off your television for a change?"

Anyway, he wouldn't meet me in the middle and choose not to listen and take responsibility and change. You can't win them all. The client has to do the work.

...you choose your life.

The above serves in part to illustrate two readily available and very modern of diseases…debt and twenty four hour, instant news coverage.

Money is only one of life's currencies, but is obviously important for many reasons, so let's have a quick chin wag about it…oh, and greed.

At this time of writing the "*World Debt*" is reaching record levels, but wait a minute… hold on, stop the bus! Who is the world in debt to? Jupiter, Mars, Pluto…Mickey Mouse? Please, do not blindly swallow this utter nonsense; I have never, ever visited any graveyard that comes complete with a cashline machine or bank. Furthermore I have never heard of a stone that transudes blood, *know what I mean?* There are limitless institutions that encourage and avail for the facilitation of debt for the masses. Please don't forget to remember that many of said organisations attract greedy psychos and sociopaths to sit at their helm. In real terms, when you are in debt to others the common two-way perception is that they own you and you are obliged to subscribe to same.

This of course is an illusion as they actually don't and you shouldn't…*all ownership is an illusion.*

- *Reframe* = all ownership is merely temporary possession.

You only have what you can hold, for as long as you can hold it.

As the world's most powerful person, *Julius Caesar* ruled most of the known world...but where is he now? The same goes for every Pharaoh, King, and Queen, ruler or very, very, very, very important person through the ages.

Furthermore, if you have more than you really need then unfortunately my friends you have *greed*. Greed is part of the disease of the modern western world and is at very the root of capitalism and commercialism. Greed is the accumulation of a stockpile of too much of anything - abstract or literal...money, food, possessions, attention, fame and is hollow on many different levels. When the Native American Indians began bartering with the first white settlers they were both bemused and amused in equal measure at the settlers desire to buy and own little pieces of the Earth, otherwise known as land. They believed that we belong to the Earth; not that it belongs to us.

The great Native American Hunkpapa Sioux holy man and warrior *Sitting Bull* observed of white European settlers in uttered words that were very similar to this;

They claim our mother, Earth for their own purpose and use. They then deface her with refuse and fence themselves off from their neighbours. They have a strange love of possessions; it is a disease in them. The white man is confused - he knows how to make everything, but does not know how to distribute it.

...not bad from a representative of what was considered a savage indigenous minority!

In many ways the Native American Indians were endowed with a concise and simplistic wisdom that put the technologically advanced settlers to shame. Once violently forced to conform and acquiesce, Sitting Bull conceded to wear conventional settler clothing, live in a small settler house on a small settler reservation...but would not, despite the best of attempts to coerce him attend church. When an exasperated reservation governor asked him why he simply replied in words like this;

I will never go to the white mans church...I wont! It only teaches them to fight about God.

Have a think on the real depth of that statement – how incisive and insightful it is in relation to most human conflicts. Once you have done so then I'd like you to have a perusal of this;

Sticklebacks

When I was a little version of me I spent endless long hot summer days fishing alone in the little stream that ran into the big stream. I sat contentedly by that little stream with my little fishing rod, with worms on my small hook. I could feel the warm ground underneath me as I sat, infinitely small on the carpet of grass.

I would gaze endlessly into the slow, steady flow...the sunlight twinkling on its translucence, tiny flies teasing it's surface...all played out to a gentle soundtrack of ripples, birdsong and breeze.

The white clouds that accompanied me formed shapes only constrained by my imagination. Those river bank times were halcyon times and, just like my books ...an escape. I can clearly remember the excitement, fascination, deep joy and satisfaction that I felt as I caught little sticklebacks by the dozen and placed them into a jam jar. I never hurt them of course; I returned them once finished - the thrill was in the chase.

Unlike some other little boys I could never ever stomach cruelty.

I recall one day one of my little friends decided to join me...he had never done it before so I showed him what to do. He didn't want to sit in the sun with me so sat in the shade underneath a large overhanging tree.

Stunningly, within seconds of his first cast he pulled a beautiful, big 2lb rainbow trout from the stream. I can vividly remember his complete shock, unbridled excitement and joy with the catch. I can vividly recall my complete and utter shock at seeing such a large, beautiful fish... and my unbridled jealousy and resentment at his stunning beginner's success.

Little Sticklebacks long forgotten I sat alone in the shade underneath that large overhanging tree for the last weeks of summer trying to catch a big 2lb rainbow trout... and never even came close.

Those halcyon times expired with the big rainbow trout... and little sticklebacks were never enough again.

I couldn't be innocent anymore because I wanted more...

In a very well known fantasy book a greedy dragon dispossessed the greedy dwarf kingdom of their immense stockpile of gold, jewels and precious items. Once he took ownership of it he contentedly slept on it under a mountain for aeons, protecting it jealously...but here's the money shot, what on earth was he going to do with it? How could a dragon possibly benefit from it? In fact...what were the dwarfs going to do with it other than covet it?

What good would it be to any of them when they were on their death bed? Anyway, some greedy dwarfs aided by an un-greedy thief eventually overcame some greedy Trolls and vanquished the greedy dragon... and then hordes of greedy Dwarfs, greedy Elves, greedy Men and greedy Orcs had a really big fight to claim ownership, oops... I mean temporary possession of it.

So, there you go – if you haven't read the book in question which features a person of small stature with large, naked, hairy feet who lives in a shire then apologies for spoiling it but now there's no need! In fairness the author doesn't need the cash anyway...

- *Be very careful - you can't take it with you...and whilst you live with greed, the things that you own, own you.*

Anyway, often *the most content people are* the ones who are not getting more...but *giving more!* The great ancient Greek philosopher Plato summed it up nicely when he asserted that *the greatest wealth in life is to live content with little*. Furthermore, please bear this in mind - the safest people to be around are the people who want nothing from anyone else.

And now, to conclude this section...24hr news.

Seeing is believing, so they all say. Magicians, mentalists and deceivers of all ilk rely on this wholly inaccurate mass held belief. The fact is of all the senses sight (as the brains preferred input system) is one of the most fallible. We have five senses – yet on average sight greedily assumes up to 60% of the brains perceptive capacity, leaving only 40% for the other four senses to argue over!

- *Reframe – Televisions are hugely powerful manipulative hypnotic tools. So much so that I call televisions Power Windows. The sender utilises the power window to manipulate the perception and unconscious world view of the receiver.*

News focuses exclusively on the tragic, unpalatable, political and negative....and this constant exposure can lead to a tragic, unpalatable, political and negative impact upon the vicarious receiver.

Have you ever wondered at the agenda of the sender responsible for which stories will be broadcast and which slant will be actively propagated? Have you ever questioned the validity or accuracy of what you are watching? *You should...always.* Also, consider this...there ARE *equally as many positive things happening in the world* as negative, yet they never quite seem to make the cut. For this reason I literally switch off and do not watch the news…

Anyway, where was I? Ah, yes back on track. There are many who believe that any *long lasting meaningful change should be* a convoluted, long, deep meaningful and painful process.

Psychologists are often guilty of this by virtue of the fact that psychology is deeply rooted with a tradition that espouses that the best way to *overcome your problem* is to first uncover it, study it and then understand it. Far be it from me to cast aspersions but let's take the deeply flawed psychoanalysis as an example. Sigmund Freud is considered one of the western worlds most influential people of the twentieth century; but did you know that Dr Freud was an abject failure as a medical practitioner and particularly fond of prescribing Cocaine to cure many mental health problems? Also you may also be interested to know that a certain other sometime close associate and early follower of Freud, Carl Jung admitted to seeking daily counsel via private conversations with an imaginary (or was it?) demon named Philemon that he considered to be his personal spirit guide?

Isn't it fascinating the interesting things come to light when you scratch beneath the veneer?

In any case this long winded problem focused approach is all fine and well if you want to invest a lot of money into your issues before finally embarking upon a protracted voyage of recovery that often never ends…however, *hellooooooo…* I am personally of the opinion that it just shouldn't be that difficult;

- *If I wanted to become better at playing the piano I wouldn't study and "understand" why an unskilled piano player plays the piano badly, just like if I wanted to feel happier I wouldn't study why a depressed person is depressed…instead I want to find out why the great piano players play so well, and why happy people are happier - and then copy that instead!*

Why study, wallow in and *"understand"* your problem when you can choose to focus instead on how the people with the opposite and reverse of your problem are doing it - *and change by just doing that instead!*

#www.justsaying.com

Perception, Projection …and Genes (not Jeans)

Percipi est esse - what is real?

Well, reality has been defined by some as the state of things as they actually exist, rather than the way in which they appear or are imagined….but is this assessment accurate?

- *Is this reality just a dream?*

Every person will believe that reality *"actually exists"* in their model of the world based upon their own subjective perception, so this begs the question…is there any such thing as any singular fixed reality at all? It is actually reasonable to consider that *all things are open to subjective interpretation,* so one persons perception of reality will be different from every other person's….to this end it can be argued that *there is actually no singular reality,* but merely our own highly individualistic interpretation of the world around us – if indeed the world around us actually exists at all!

Let's take it even one step further, once understood it becomes clear that one of the basic tenets of quantum physics is that we are not simply experiencing reality…*we are actively involved in its creation!* The nature of reality is that it is participatory.

- *You may not be actually living in the real world; you could be living in an elaborate representation of it, one that you have formed within your brain.*

After all, all experiences are merely electronic impulses received by the brain – it converts sensory input into a code of frequencies. The codification is the core language of an eclectic cybernetic electromagnetic sentient being…i.e. *you*.

More on this…*soon!*

Eugene

Whilst visiting hospital several times a week for several weeks at a time I couldn't help but notice an old man in the bed opposite the bed I was visiting. At first he was constantly asleep, and then he was awake.

Spare and fit looking for his age it turned out he was 92 years young and his hands weren't following the script anymore. He liked to talk and we did. He revealed; "I was a great golfer, I played off a 2 par. After my wife died I lived for golf…I played almost every day until quite recently." He let out a sigh and with a glazed look further revealed; "My biggest sadness is that I can no longer play golf. I loved the breeze on my skin, the fresh air in my lungs and the beautiful scenery…the feel of the club in my hands as I hit the ball" I replied "I can grasp what you are saying…but pardon me… of course you can… in fact, why not have a round tonight?"

I met a puzzled look, so expanded;

"All you have to do is close your eyes, feel the breeze on your skin, taste and smell the fresh air in your lungs, hear the birds and enjoy the beautiful scenery once again. Feel the club in your hand and hit the ball once more. Immerse yourself. It's just as real as reality. Have a round tonight on the course in your head"

He thought on that awhile, and then gave me the thumbs up.

The following day he had perked up and told me that he had enjoyed a wonderful round of golf in the privacy of his head that night and that he planned to have another that night. He said to me "You are a good man" – which was confirmation that he was indeed.

It takes one to know one.

The pictures and movies that you create inside are in many ways as real as the internal sounds and voice that you hear. Maximise and enhance the good ones and shrink the opposite or reverse. Get rid of the obscene graffiti in your mind – paint over it, let it go…get rid of it! *Immerse yourself into the powerful cognitive imagery that you can generate…it is as real as the alternative.*

You may believe that you perceive the external world (*reality*) as it is, but *you have* actually *represented, absorbed and coded all of the things that you have touched, seen, heard, smelled* and *tasted* through *your bespoke mind filtering system*; and have subsequently projected your internal reality upon the external world.

All information is unconsciously filtered through our *Meta Programs* (basis of personality), *Beliefs, Decisions, Attitudes, Memories, Values and Language* – we then *Delete, Distort and Generalise* this information. If you'd like more information on this then look up the NLP mind filtration system.

Anyway, the resultant perception of what is the external reality is merely a reflection of that individual subjective reality which has been assimilated, formulated and then adopted internally. Now, I know this may be a bit of a mental stretch but just hang in there as it is worth processing and understanding the following;

The concept of *Perception is Projection* operates on the basic premise that we *cannot not* project our ideas, our values, attitudes, models, understandings and judgments' upon other people, objects and things...*you just can't can not do it.*

You look at yourself when you look at others; that's why we like people who are like us.

This is much like the concept of self fulfilling beliefs...that is, we unconsciously seek external verification of our beliefs via confirmation bias – and we subsequently always find it.

What really? Yes, really.

We either like those who are like us or possess traits or abilities what we would like to have. *Birds of a feather and all that!* Further to this, until recently the scientific community asserted that the human body contained up to 2 million genes; and that these genes largely determined the basis of the personality.

There has however been a very important shift - it is now scientifically accepted that there are only approximately 25,000 genes; and that genetics alone do not in fact have quite the same impact upon the wholeness of a person as was previously believed. Science is indeed limited by the parameters of current knowledge; it is reasonable to now consider that the personality is determined to a much larger degree within the mind and within ones formative environmental circumstance than had ever been thought possible. Each person therefore experiences and is highly influenced by significant others during their non-critical imprint period and mentally *decides* upon the way in which they will be and behave.

The basis of your personality is also the result of your upbringing and environment – much less your genetics.

Although heavily influenced by their parents, siblings etc *the basis of personality is* ultimately the prerogative and *choice of the individual;*

- *You physically originate from your parents…but you are not your parents or their parents…or theirs. You are you and you are original. That body and mind of yours is yours.*

So, here is the thing - *you can be whoever you want to be,* and you should be as you wish to seem.

Often during interpersonal and observational vicarious interactions *you will find only those preconceived things which you unconsciously expect to find in others*; importantly you can only find that which is already attributed to, and constituted within your own ego and psyche. These findings will often fundamentally be unconsciously unresolved personal issues;

- *Be careful what you say of others…it is what you say of yourself!*

I know you are but what am I?

He was strong but was weak. I knew he had self confidence issues as he never had a nice word to say about anybody. Anyway physical strength, ego, power and greed impress me much less than kindness, generosity, integrity and humility.

He once assessed me and sneered "You're not very good at that, are you?" and I looked him up and down and replied "Are you sure I'm not not good at it, am I actually not that?"

He then blurted "The things you say are stupid…you are stupid!" to which I blurted "Esse est precipi - I know you are but what am I?" He then replied "You are an idiot!"

…I adopted a slightly bashful posture and stated with complete sincerity and humility "thanks very much for the compliment, I really appreciate

it!" The fact I took his insult as a compliment confused him so he had one more try; "Are you always this stupid?!?!" and I said "I am that stupid only always once three or four times a month as long as there is a half crescent full moon!" Not knowing how to deal with that he stormed off and troubled me not again.

Sticks and stones will break component elements of my vertebral skeleton...but words will never hurt me! A wise man taught me that if someone sets out to hurt your feelings and you choose to let them succeed to then walk with haste to the nearest bin and dump them.

Never, ever take an insult from anyone; always leave it with the insulter. It is actually their problem...

I recommend you don't *process the previous tale*; it isn't very important. Others will often attempt to hurt your feelings – protect yourself with the following simple attitude;

> If you decide not to be hurt > then you will not feel hurt > If you do not feel hurt > then you haven't been hurt!

- *Reframe - When you realise that the other person's behaviour towards you is actually a reflection of their relationship with themselves then you will find that you barely even feel like reacting at all.*

Although we can never truly perceive the world as others do, I have always found that it is healthy to take the time to walk in the moccasins of others when appropriate. Stepping into their position and a third that is neutral enables us to adopt an entirely different perceptual position of any situation. This allows us to mentally view/preview/review any situation from a number of quite different perspectives. This always leads to an enriched insight and new appreciation …and facilitates a greater understanding of others. Wisdom is born of multiple perspectives.

Perceptual position exercise;

The next time you are involved in an interpersonal interaction with another actively carry out the following.

- Adopt the first position, your own.

In this position you will look at the world from your own point of view. It is easy to do as you have probably been doing this for your entire life. In this place you will be totally associated (seeing things through your own eyes, feeling things as you are, hearing what you hear.)

In this position think about how things affect you.

- Adopt the second position, the other persons.

Step into the other person's skin and find yourself looking at yourself from their point of view. In the position give consideration for how the other person looks at the situation, how they feel, what they hear. In this position you open up a profound appreciation from their point of view…how things appear to them.

- Adopt the third position (Meta).

Now adopt the position of being completely neutral. Step out of both your own and the other persons skin and inhabit another space in the room. In this position you are dissociated from the first two perspectives and are able to have a holistic overview of the interaction. Become an independent observer. In this position you open up a valuable perspective…how it looks to someone not involved.

The key to this exercise is to be acutely aware that all three positions are equally important, and that you should be flexible and best able to move freely between them at will…taking all that you have gained from each with you of course!

The above exercise is incredibly powerful and enlightening, with a little cognitive practice you will find yourself being able to carry it out during virtually any interaction. With practice you will find that it empowers you with an objectivity that enables for useful choices and evaluations in difficult relationships or situations.

Make no mistake, the ability to *see things from multiple perspectives* is a *key skill in understanding* other *people*, and facilitates an ever more effective communication process in relationships, negotiations, meetings and interviews. Most of us are quick to judge others, and others will usually be equally quick to judge you – but remember this;

- *The only judgment you should ever accept of yourself should be that judgment that you alone have made…*

Following a conversation with his demonic spirit guide (probably…hey, I'm not judging!) Carl Jung asserted that you cannot judge another to have a certain aspect, or archetype within their persona without having it within your own….and projecting it upon them in much the same way as you would cast a veritable shadow in the midday sun. So, when you make an assessment that another is annoying, troublesome, aggressive, angry, and stupid or otherwise you are actually identifying an identical negative part of yourself. This theory also of course applies to the identification of positive traits…so never forget to remember to look for the best in people, *play nice …and be kind to yourself!*

Perception is projection is akin to looking in a proverbial mirror and casting your gaze upon a reflection of your own self!

So to summarise;

For an individual to be able to recognise an aspect of another person's character they must have ownership of the very same inherent characteristic, i.e. if you did not have the same trait you would be unable to recognise it in the first instance.

- *You cannot recognise what you do not know.*

See things through the eyes of others and others other than others to attain new wisdom and perspective. Once you have truly done that you will be best able to judge yourself. The combination of a higher perspective we leave you less inclined to accept the cursory judgments of others, or others other than others.

Capeesh…?

Self Image, Confidence…Trust

People are often their own worst critic, and as such we are all quite proficient in the seedy dark art of self-sabotage;

Life is a rollercoaster

Life is like a rollercoaster, sometimes it comes off the rails. When is does often all that can be done is neither much, little nor meaningful…however can we only ever do no more than our best at any point in time?

Once the dust begins to settle then we often hurt ourselves with recriminations of our inability to take control…we tell ourselves "I should have been more…"

In fact we are usually just another victim of the rollercoaster and can not be more; we should enjoy the highs, endure the lows …and get out of the way when the rails come off.

In a moment… pay attention now… this is insight; climb back onboard, have a quiet word with yourself and decide to cut you some slack….

Ah, good old self communication - do you remember us discussing that discussion with yourself earlier during the introduction to this book what seemed like only yesterday all my troubles seemed so far away?

A person at this point may or may not revisit that or not…

Inner dialogue is immensely powerful, so immensely powerful that it has a dramatic influence upon how we perceive ourselves, achieve results…or not as the case may or may not be. We have already covered the incessant thoughts that never ever cease during the waking state unless you cultivate mental discipline through *mindlessness*, or *mind guidance*. Well, here's the thing, from the moment you awake until the moment you fall asleep you also constantly generate internal dialogue inside your head! As you read this you are converting the collection of letters into a linguistic auditory representation inside.

So…what does your internal voice sound like?

Have you ever even taken the time to pay attention to it, its volume, location, tonality, cadence, timbre? Please do so now, after all, what have you got to lose mi amigo?

- *You are always talking away to yourself. Always. Have you noticed?*

Not only do you do it…every person does it. We all use self talk –

it's a highly pervasive and significant part of our two fold self communication process! The second part of this process is self image – the visualised internal perception that you form and hold of yourself in your mind. So, your internal self-talk and self image form your self communication which in turn will shape your feelings and emotions regarding that which you are, your self-worth and personal esteem. This is all great and good; well I should say…it could *be great and good*. The fact is that most of us have a tendency for unsupportive, even detrimental use of this inherent cognitive activity to undermine the self and impede, even damage our own greater good.

With self dialogue we principally do this in the following ways;

- Sentiments and statements of <u>Despair</u> – these are consisted of the type of dialogue that consists of on-going negativity, thoughts that presuppose that *there is* no *point in attempting* or *persisting* with a certain course of *action* because *there is always* no *hope* of success or attainment.

- Sentiments and statements of <u>Powerlessness</u> – these consist of the self-defeating things that you say to yourself that inform you that *you do* not *have sufficient ability to achieve better*. This type of self-talk renders *you*, the individual much less capable and willing to *take action*.

- Sentiments and statements of <u>Deficiency</u> – These are the things that we say internally to ourselves that inform us that *we* don't *deserve* any *better* than that which we have *in our lives* or our results.

I personally know some people who have not only been bullied by their own internal dialogue…they have been perpetually tortured by cruel, unforgiving self-talk. Why criticize and put yourself down? It is counterproductive, totally unreasonable and feeds low self-esteem. You should always *be your own best friend!* I have a nice and easy technique for fixing this – when you become aware of it and want it to stop simply follow this advice and apply this technique;

Gently bite your tongue between you front teeth (seriously, try it) then internally say in a loud assertive manner;

> *"Would the part of me that is being unsupportive to my wellbeing*
>
> *SHUT UP!!!! SHUT UP!!!! SHUT UP!!! SHUT UP!!!!"*

Ahem…just saying. Add some fucking swear words if *it helps grab your fucking attention*. After all, you are driving the bus and are actually in charge. *That internal voice is you* and *you are it*, so decide to *change it* and stop fucking hurting yourself.

Assume control.

Your internal voice can be anything you want it to be…as can your self image. If you actually knew the sheer volume of beautiful people walking around with a desperately poor, even ugly internal self image you may be shocked. You become what you think. Consider the life impact upon a beautiful person with an ugly, distorted image of themselves – think of the far reaching impact upon their life. Someone who holds a negative self image and is plagued by negative self-talk will never feel worthy, will accept low standards and surround themselves with much less than they deserve.

Beauty is subjective, however have you ever noticed a beautiful person walking arm in arm with an unattractive partner and wondered *"What's that all about??? He/She could do so much better!!"* – Well, this can mean all manner of things; however I guarantee at least two possible principle reasons are at play;

- *It could be that the unattractive partner either has lots of money, some fabulous, witty badinage, lovely personality…or maybe the beautiful partner does not recognise and appreciate their own beauty and has resultant low standards.*

Make your self-image and internal voice supportive and play nice; there are enough assholes out there that will gladly accept any opportunity to put you down.

- *Be kind to yourself. In fact go one better…love yourself. You cannot hate yourself into being something that you will love*

A strong self image undoubtedly feeds confidence, and now I will discuss that very state of being because it is often greatly misunderstood;

Everybody wants confidence, but the paradox is that confidence is in itself absolutely free – regardless as to whether or not it is warranted or deserved. What does that mean? Well, it means this;

There are lots and lots of people out there walking around with super levels of confidence that they have helped themselves to and adopted without sufficient investment or capability. These people are often blissfully unaware that they have built their castle upon shifting sands!

This is their equation;

> CONFIDENCE + competence = <u>Overconfidence</u> = unbalance

Overconfident people often tend to be full of their own drivel, importance, boorish, overbearing …and very boring!

Equally I have known of some very competent people who have suffered from a complete lack of confidence.

This is theirs;

> COMPETENCE + confidence = <u>Diffidence</u> = unbalance

Those with diffidence are actually much better company; they are blessed with doubt, which actually can be a virtue.

Their modesty and shyness often proving to be endearing and attractive character traits…but the big problem is that they do not usually meet their potential, which in real terms is a pity!

In actual fact real, meaningful confidence equates to this;

> COMPETENCE + CONFIDENCE = <u>balance</u>

Origins of confidence;

> *Confidence* – *based on the Latin "Com Fidere"*
>
> *Com = "to put emphasis on" + Fidere = "To have self faith",*
>
> *Thus confidence = "Emphasis on faith in oneself."*

So, what is the moral of the story?

Well, here's my top tip…if you want more confidence then become more competent – this does not mean that you will have no doubts…but remember uncertainty can be a prime motivator. In this way your castle will be built upon a solid, concrete foundation and the walls of it will be patrolled by an adept guard. Get better at whatever you do, practice, rehearse and learn. Practice is the mother of all success.

Once again…be *open to meaningful feedback.*

Do not be afraid to make mistakes…after all each one is but a mere lesson within itself, and every lesson my friends makes you better. Indeed, often failure is the first step to success.

Know your subject matter as a matter of course, after all;

- *If your confidence is not based upon actual accomplishment…then what is it based upon?*

Trust is another anomalous state. People tend to think in the terms of all or nothing when it comes to trust, i.e. you either trust someone or you don't. This type of thinking is flawed, as trust can be much better applied by way of sliding continuum scale;

1 2 3 4 5 6 7 8 9 10

Not trusted ……………………….Trusted

So think on this; a person may be quite trustworthy – say a 6/10 on the sliding scale. This person despite being really quite trustworthy still actually has room for slippage if you think in the way of the sliding scale. *All or Nothing* thinking of *Trustworthy* or *Not to be Trusted* does not…and in this case the person you deemed *Trusted* may shock you by letting you down. If you have a tendency to be too trusting you can be defined as *Axial*!

If you are this way inclined then, sorry to be the bearer of bad news…you are the *actual* targets of every scammer, from Nigerian email Princes seeking to have funds released to the guy that turns up on your doorstep informing you that you have a loose roof tile and he can fix it for a "fair" price!

You may also decree that another person is *Not to be Trusted*…perhaps a 2/10 or so, but once again application of the sliding scale will allow for this person to perhaps surprise you by coming up trumps! Those who lack trust in others can be defined as *Marginal*! For you good news; The Nigerian email Prince and dodgy tradesman do not expect to get any joy from you whatsoever.

So, now, here's a question - how many people will you ever be likely to meet who you will grade to be a 10/10...*including you?* Can you even trust yourself completely? If you're completely honest the answer will be... *no*. People let themselves down all the time.

I don't trust anybody completely, including myself because I have let myself down on more than one occasion...but I grade others by using the sliding scale. It is after all more flexible and realistic.

- *By applying this in your life nobody will ever completely surprise you by letting you down!*

The Body Eclectic...the Body Electric

The ghost in the machine

A person may or may not wonder if a human being is actually a spiritual being currently having a human experience...

...whether or not you are, are not, think you are, think that you are not or neither think you are or are not there is one thing that is seemingly absolute - you have your very own body. It is completely unique and there is no other just like it anywhere; proof of this is readily available....just lift your hand and check out the intricacy of your fingerprints or the lines on the palm of your hand;

The four leaved Clover

As a child my eldest daughter was curious to know; one day she found a large patch of clover in the woods. Excitedly, she tried to search for a four leaved version amongst the large cluster. What seemed like hours were spent on hands and knees in her patient, determined search... and as you may imagine, she began to be aware of the lack thereof...

When she was done I inquired "And, what did you discover?" To which she replied "I started to notice that each one is slightly different from the other!"

The more you search the more you do tend to find. Part of her uniqueness is that she is always curious to know...and she did a good job.

Now, it's fair to say that you the reader are undoubtedly currently having a real live human experience in your very own custom body – that is as it should be;

The Difference that makes a difference

When I was a younger version of me I was acutely aware of being different, and it was very uncomfortable.

Then I grew up and I was acutely aware of being different, and it was very comforting.

It's good to be comfortable...

You might as well know something else at this juncture; your body is not only a universal, quantum mechanical device, it also has a self generated, subtle energy field.

It is even visible with the naked eye.

"He's finally lost it!" you may or may not exclaim! But I haven't.

Don't believe me? *Have a look...a really good look.* All it takes is the conscious effort to expand upon your visual sense. It may well be that you have always seen it but deleted it. I can see subtle energy fields around people and inanimate objects, I always have. It is mostly much like a translucent silhouetted glow. Sometimes a faint colour is perceivable. This type of perception is conventionally termed in our modern world as paranormal, supernormal or just plain weird - but it isn't; it's normalnormal. As a species we just have a very limited understanding of nature. Interestingly some people's aura glows more than others. Hmmmm, now why is that I wonder?

- *You are an electromagnetic being. Everything you do is enabled by electrical signals.*

How is this so? Well, *everything in the universe is made of subatomic particles* and *atoms*, and atoms my friends are made of neutrons, electrons and protons. Neutrons have a neutral electronic charge; electrons have a negative charge, and protons have a positive charge. When these charges are out of balance then an atom becomes positively or negatively charged, and this allows for electrons to flow from one atom to another...and this folks is electricity. Its simple *Electron(ics)*

And so, as we are a massive collection of atoms we thus generate a fair old bit of electricity. We ingest food, it is broken down on a molecular, elemental level in a process called *cellular respiration*, and these molecules and elements have the capacity to be used as *electron(ic)* impulses as required by the body.

This fact has been known by modern medical science for a long time. You see, just as doctors utilise *electroencephalograms* to record the electrical activity of the brain, they also use *electrocardiographs* to measure the electrical activity of the heart and *electromyography* to measure the electrical activity of the muscles…and, wait for it, more recently to also gauge the electrical human *energy field*, or for those of a new age persuasion the *Aura*.

This energy field has been found to have the potential for a very wide range of frequencies which is gauged as *Cycles per Second (cps)*, or, ahem, for those of a new age persuasion *vibrations*. Of course different mental activity actually has a significant impact upon the *cps*, or *vibration* (remember the mind affects the body and the body affects the mind!) For example, focus on materialistic, worldly, kinaesthetic bodily function typically results in an average range in the region of 250*cps*, yet trance, meditative and spiritual states such as prayer can reach up to 900*cps*. Some of the most extreme and rare readings have astoundingly been graded in the range of 200,000*cps*!

Would *you be surprised* to know that what are the strongest recorded parts of the energy field centre of parts of the body traditionally associated with what the ancients called Chakras? This begs another question…how can we explain how ancient spiritual traditions have espoused the Chakras many hundreds of years before it has been scientifically proven?

I actually don't know, do you? *Answers on a postcard please to;*

#www.wtf.com.net.uk

As *you can imagine,* I'm not exactly sure how new *knowledge* of such mostly unseen aspects could *enable a person* to be able *to develop new understandings now,* or how this type of phenomenon can be useful or not to the casual observer…however the more I ponder that the more I *ponder it. You* don't have to *think about it,* but being a person means being a human being ...and being. And all that being said it's always been a good idea to... *just be.*

Anyway, this has now become the chapter that then was.

What's next I wonder...?

4 CONTEMPLATIONS

In a mercurial way I always sometimes *enjoy* a few snatched *moments of* profound observational reflection…*contemplation*. Things often resonate deeply within me; I think differently, it's the way I'm wired. I do also like to *imagine things* too; *you* may *notice you* can *imagine* that *too*…

For some reason I'm an abstract thinker and naturally tend to make obscure connections as opposed to the conventional; this mostly happens quite randomly when I least expect it. What about you? Do you think it's good to think thoughts that *connect to higher, lower or hidden aspects of you, other things or to nothing at all?* Such is my affliction, as a child I remember becoming cerebrally frustrated by the fact that the *"How much is that doggy in the window?"* rhyme never actually revealed the actual cost. So, as you can realise I contemplate the macroscopic, the microscopic, the sublime and the ridiculous *you know*?

This includes other things like;

- *If dogs could smile would they wag their tails?*
- *Why people don't realise that if domestic cats were 4 times bigger would they hunt us instead of mice!*

- *Has nobody else apart from me noticed that people are unable to talk as they inhale?*
- *The way people always reveal their thinking process through unconscious eye movement and body language*
- *If vampires cast no reflection why is their hair always perfect?*
- *Why in this digital, mostly non superstitious age the days of the week are named after three planets (The Sun, Saturn and The Moon) and four mythological Norse gods (Tiaw, (W)Oden, Thor and Freyja)*
- *Why my nose hair grows four times faster than the hair on my head?*

And that's just for starters.

Don't get me started on the divine, the universe, plants & trees (*do they have feelings?*), atoms, the collective biological cellular amalgamations that form large objects called humans, the planet, its population and how we, people are in complete control of all we survey as supremely powerful masters of the Earth, virtual technological demigods in our own right. After all don't we have weapons that could destroy life on Earth and thus have the ultimate power to create and destroy everything?

Indeed, and we are even capable of (and actively significantly invest on many different levels) the launch of reconnaissance spacecraft to explore outer space, the ultimate exploration of our physical boundaries; yet we seem much less interested in exploring our vast, unexplored inner space.

Now, why is that? In any case all of the aforementioned underlines and consolidates our species universal importance, does it not? After all, we are in *complete control*...aren't we?

Well....actually, no.

- This amounts to no more than a quite delusional and misleading human self deception – *mostly to ease our collective primate reptilian brain reactionary fear response of not actually being so.*

As a species we are collectively guilty of it, burying those ultimate truths which are unpalatable or hard to digest in conceptual shallow graves that occupy only the fringes of our consciousness. We overestimate ourselves completely and utterly in what is no more than an egotistical grand deception. If the truth be known no person is ever in complete control of themselves…*not even close*…so how can they be in complete control of anything else including such grand designs as the aforementioned universals? This is evident in body language, which in contrary to carefully premeditated use of language on a conscious level is usually an *honest unconscious display of what is really happening inside;*

If someone's verbal language is contrary to their non verbal communication *always believe their body language.* Only recently I watched a very high profile Scottish politician during a televised interview assert that *"This is absolutely in the best interests for Scotland!"* – more revealing however was her body language…she was shaking her head side to side whilst saying it!

Take from that what you will, but her conscious use of language was being overridden by her unconscious …and *the unconscious is the true reflection, not only the powerful part of the mind, but also the honest, virtually unhindered part.* Physiological displays disclose what is really happening inside. Carefully watch others and you will see this phenomenon a lot! Oh, and whilst I'm perched up here on my soapbox here is something else to put into your contemplative pipe and smoke – why is it that the older and wiser you become the more that it appears that *everyone else is* actually *winging it? Contemplate that.* Answers on an epostcard to;

#www.thatsbecausetheyactuallyare.com.co.uk.net

Do you really think that no one else shares all of those insecurities, those feelings of inadequacy those feelings of not being quite good enough? Think again. Some are better are reconciling themselves to them and hiding them better than others. *How good are you* at it?

So, in reference to my original point, once more lurking in the closet is the prime mover and shaker - good old bad old *fear*.

Let's get real for a moment - if we detonated every weapon of mass destruction upon each other in an attempt to destroy all life the actual impact upon this *seemingly* fragile Earth would be akin in relative terms to gently denting the skin of an apple with a badly bitten finger nail…barely a veritable scratch upon the surface! Life forms at microcosmic levels wouldn't even notice that anything significant had happened and the Earth would very quickly get over us, *regenerate… and move on.*

- *Human life as we perceive it could finally cease for all time and the Universe probably wouldn't notice or actually really give a shit!*

Brace yourself…but I'm of the emotionally based opinion that the Universe doesn't feel any particular love for us. Have you noticed that things rarely just fall nicely into place? In the vague notion that the universe was resisting all of my best efforts I used to curse the fact that things rarely went easy for me or just fell into line; in time I came to realise that it didn't even notice or care either way …and that for things to go right I actually had to make them happen. It's just the nature of things. Now, my previous assertion appears cold but please understand this *very important* additional factor - the universe doesn't actually feel loathe for us or feel anything in between for us either!

It is most likely neither benevolent nor malevolent…it is

primordial *and just is.* Anyway, remember that we are composed of the same subatomic particles as everything else in the universe and are therefore one and the same with it. Ergo we are an infinitesimally small chip off the old block so to speak; *we are the universe.*

Science & the Spiritual

Scientists would assert that the vast and incomprehensibly complex universe quite randomly just came into being – but despite finding science fascinating I just can't completely subscribe to that. Have a look at your current mobile phone of choice and tell me, has that just come into being? Do incomprehensibly complex things really just come into being from nothing? *Contemplate that…*and this; Religious leaders would assert that one cannot look at the stars in the night sky and deny or question the divine omnipotence and magnificence of a supreme beings creation – but despite an intense feeling of the divine, an intense feeling that I am a spiritual being I can't completely subscribe to that either. Without any tangible proof whatsoever is it unreasonable for a rational, objective, inquiring mind not to at least question such?

Can the absence of evidence be evidence of the absence? I wonder…

One of the problems with science is that it attempts to explain that which the spiritual can not. One of the problems with the spiritual is that it attempts to explain that which science cannot. *Contemplate that!*

And so, all of this is fascinating, and as a contemplator makes me even *more curious…* but the more I understand the less I know.

It does seem to be a bit of a double bind!

Population & Learning

Now, the current head count at this time of writing with regard to this small, moist lump of rock which is gently rotating through the solar system at 460 metres per second and 1,000 miles an hour, precisely located approximately exactly somewhere in infinity and time stands at around 7 and a half thousand million…or 7.5 Billion in layman's terms.

Bear in mind that in the year 1800 the world population was approximately one thousand million, or 1 Billion – so, the population has increased over sevenfold in the space of 200 years!

This means that the planet is full, space is at a premium, resources are running out at a rate that is concerning the world leaders of the western world and as a consequence we are all completely screwed.

Are you scared yet?

Well, oh contraire, let me whisper loudly an unspoken secret…*you actually shouldn't be.* At this point I will clarify that proportion can only ever be contextualised in relative terms of one thing to another in comparative terms; the fact of the matter is;

- *This planet is actually really GIGANTIC in relation to its human population (which is in fact on the cusp of a major population downturn, look it up!) And in any case actually remains largely unpopulated; ergo there are actually more than enough resources for everyone.*

…so *relax*. You see, I set you up a moment ago by writing "*This small moist lump or rock"* and *"the planet is full"* and *"Resources are running out"* a few moments ago...ahem, a small exploitation in relative terms in comparison to the pervasive, insidious exploitation of the reactionary primate fear response of the masses by the supposed great and good.

Don't get me wrong, those theories that espouse convoluted conspiracies at every turn make me chuckle; from personal experience I would say that most significant organisations or elite groups are barely even able to agree on what type of biscuit to have with their tea ...never mind masterminding the artful concealment of downed alien spacecraft, the three eyed lizard people from Jupiter who really built the pyramids, the remnants of Atlantis and actively orchestrating Machiavellian world domination plans. *Just saying.....*

Oh, and before I forget, and whilst I'm on the topic of the three eyed lizard men from Jupiter responsible for building the pyramids, am I the only one who finds it strange that all of mankind's invented monsters and aliens are based on hominoid automorphism? Seeing things in a distorted, twisted (or otherwise) versions of our own image does betray a lack of true creative imagination don't *you think?* I mean, why would an alien from Jupiter look like a lizard or have a head, legs, arms, claws or any eyes at all? Would it not be more likely to look like nothing we could even comprehend? *Contemplate that.*

How and ever, don't mind me...

One thing many of our world leaders have been driving hard for is Globalisation.

It appears to be a newish concept fed by technological advances, and it is true this has dramatically sped the process up ...however globalisation is in no way a new concept. Now, I don't actually intend to argue for or against globalisation in this text, I will leave that to those who have actually benefitted from a "deesent skool edukashion" – but I will say this…during my contemplations the modern phenomenon of globalisation seems to lead to one particular puzzle wrapped up in an enigma. It has created a new age paradox that is this;

- *The more connected we are becoming in a localised, integrated world the more isolated it seems we are becoming from each other, our surroundings and more worryingly still…from ourselves.*

Skool Edukation

At school, as a younger version of me, I was in touch with and… fully absorbed…in a world that was twice the size. After all I was only half the size back then in that uncomfortable classroom; I excelled at only one thing…trance.

Trapped, I would gaze longingly out of the window and pass those old school days by releasing my imagination to roam free…whilst going deeper inside…then.

One frustrated teacher once scornfully scolded me "You will never amount to anything at all"…as a shy, awkward but willful Virgo I said "Miss. You have your opinion, but I have my own!"…after all, I had Mars in Leo, and the potential to live my life the way I wanted to…

Don't get me wrong, my choice then was to set low academic expectations, which in fairness I never failed to meet…however if the learner cannot learn in the way the teacher teaches the teacher needs to learn to teach in the way that the learner will learn.

Despite innate inattentiveness I didn't let my education get in the way of my learning and the lessons that I received actually taught me how to teach others. In truth good teachers teach, bad teachers don't …but great teachers inspire!

The reality is that nobody can ever amount to nothing. Nothing is something after all. You see, you can't lose if ...you adopt the right attitude ... you can only ever win or learn.

...the lessons of failure taught me much.

There is no failure, only feedback and as *you know feedback is never the end* unless you renounce it or quit.

The secret of success is to *never give up on worthwhile goals* and learn your lessons well. So, as you and I are talking about learning why not become comfortable because I want to share a short story. It'll only take about 240 seconds or so;

The Tree house

My good old friend and I were very lucky young people in so many ways. We grew up in the country and had the kind of freedom that only a couple of daft young boys, like we were, could take for granted. It's funny the things that you have – and don't know that you have...until you know now. He was a quiet boy, some considered him a bit strange, so much so that even he considered himself strange – but we went together like chips and fish. He was the brains of the operation and I was the muscle. Small, thin, quiet and pensive, he could tell you the square route of an orange – but he couldn't peel it! Girls would laugh at him – never a good thing for a young man. That's were I came in. I was tall, strong, athletic, practical and good looking back then.

I benefit from strong Viking genes after all....but then you know that. Did you ...know that... the Vikings learned how to navigate by using the stars...indeed, aiming for the stars... in their tiny longboats?

They undoubtedly did learn through experience...by trying...never giving up...being brave. And they got there in the end....wherever there was...going far...in the end.

And they did. But I digress. We decided to build a tree house one hot summer. I recall it was an ancient, huge old Oak tree that reached for the sky....with a lot of powerful branches full of colourless green leaves, and it was grounded, with strong, deep roots. My granddad taught me how to build things from wood by doing so...and I could...and would...I was good. Having a good teacher makes a difference.... you know it? I had to teach him because he didn't even know, then, how to hold a hammer. At first he was frustrated and told me "It's not fair, I can't do practical things because I'm just not practical!"...but I laughed, because sometimes people take life too seriously....life should be fun too...and we two had fun learning too to do what we wanted to get a tree house for two too. And to get what you want you have to persevere, and overcome difficulties....like the Vikings did. I taught my good old pal how to build a tree house in the end because even though he was clever....like you are ...he had to learn new things...and there are so many ways to learning things is easy. But you have learned already all about that...but maybe you have forgotten what you know you knew that anyway...because, and here is the secret... everyone is clever in their own way and can learn new things like my good old pal....easily. An elephant never forgets what it knows because elephants never forget...maybe people never forget about the things that they know...deep, deep, down....but often they think they have, and they become scared. But there is a safe place...that protects you...inside. You won't fail...because there is no fail...only feedback. And I have learnt to love feedback, because feedback is a gift from others who are especially good at doing something that makes you better at doing those things! He learnt how to use a hammer that hot summer, and built that tree house back then with me....thanks to my granddad, who taught me how to teach him. Sure, he ended up with a splinter or two, but such is life. Nothing in life comes without some price or other, and the path to achievement is often littered with small failures. Generations pass on these things. And in turn he taught me how to teach...you...and others. I am grateful to him for that because even though I came from brawny Viking stock I learnt that I was clever...in a different way from him...but clever all the

133

same. And my granddad also taught him, through me…to learn and to believe all things are possible.

I found out recently that my mother's, mother's husband had a huge IQ and was touted by the very finest universities… but couldn't go because his family needed him to tend to the farm to help feed his many, hungry siblings, a sacrifice he was willing to make. Sometimes we can't have want we want. He knew hunger…and died hungry a short time after the tree house had been completed. But the marks he made are still ingrained. The remnants of that tree house are still there…on that ancient oak tree…the rusty old nails deeply embedded…maybe for all time….I remember that I had almost forgotten what I have now remembered. My pal did a good job of putting them there. Who would have thought he would have the confidence to go on to be so highly sought after and respected…so successful…so admired.

That boy did know how to learn…

So, take that lesson… from me to you, it's free.

I'd also like you to learn this before *you progress* any *further* - Globalisation can be guilty of stoking the flames of unconscious mass fear; it is often the catalyst behind the "Small world, too many people, no space, resource running out" proverbial cattle feed. Why create this illusion? Well, partly because if *"The people"* are kept off balance and anxious then they are more easily controlled. Have you also noticed that most political parties have an election time rhetoric consisting of subtle yet subversive and malevolent fear mongering? It's a timeless ploy; create a climate of fear so that you can then paint yourself as the solution and alternative for said fear…sit back, and count the votes! Continual repetition of falsehoods can amount to what becomes a war of attrition - one that facilitates for acceptance, obedience and absorption. Our personal values are the things that are of most importance to us and I always question the values of significant politicians and analyse their real agenda's, it helps to push beneath the veneer - *you* may *begin to* too. After all, it's wise to beware the (wo)man who would be king (or queen) - especially the type of dog that chews upon other dogs.

Secondly, always never forget to remember this… *"The people"* actually do like to be scared, don't you? It breaks the day up; you know…the monotony of a mundane life. It is why we ride roller coasters, bungee/parachute jump, celebrate Halloween, smoke drugs, inject drugs, inhale drugs, eat drugs, drink drugs, tell ghost stories, break speed limits when driving, watch horror movies and are strangely attracted at various times in our lives to risk! Why? Allow me to refer you to the familiar term *"Adrenaline Junkie"* – that is, facing fearful situations and surviving gives us a massive neurological chemical dump; deposited directly into our cellular system it can feel surprisingly intoxicating …and is therefore addictive!

- *Now a word to the wise; if at this juncture it all appears quite appealing … much like a candle that burns brightly then quickly expires adrenaline junkies tend to live fast and die young.*

And that is of course your choice; after all some people would actually rather go out with a loud bang than slowly fade away but, hey wait…we've done this already in the Life section!

Anyway, as you are currently still here, there, wherever you are and still reading this you should know that continual fear causes continual stress …and this is not good for the old grey matter. In fact it changes the physical structure, size and the effective functionality of the brain. Make no mistake; significant physical and chemical changes take place in the brain in relation to the way in which an individual thinks with regards neural pathways and networking. For example stress begins neurologically within the Hypothalamus Pituitary Adrenal Axis which is the stimulant (along with the Kidney) of *Cortisol* release, stimulating the *Amygdala* (the brains fear management centre) and thus the primeval reptilian brain fight, flight or freeze response – all of this weakens the *Hippocampus* (the learning/fear control centre of the brain) and literally damages synaptic connections.

As you can imagine too much continual fear and stress can have many associated serious, long lasting health implications; heart problems, kidney issues, eczema, constipation…I could go on. So *relax people!*

Relax…

A skeptical man said "I can't afford treatment, it's too expensive" and I said "Can you afford not to? Many people have found making the investment in themselves to be an expense that was worth every penny spent!"

He thought about that and then replied "Well, I have chronic constipation and need help.

I hold onto things and have such hard problems…I just can't let go of these things. Life is so, so hard; things just never go easy for me." I said "Shit! You may… pooh, pooh …now…what I say… but soften up, relax…now…just… re….lax! That and those things may seem hard, but nothing actually lasts forever …know this…all these things will pass!" Which he did, and his constipation was gone.

*…you see, to relax is to become less tense or anxious, and the act of relaxing comprises; **re**(visit) something that has often been done before and **lax**(ative) which is to soften.*

…people do tend to vastly underrate the way in which words can make things happen!

Now, whether all of the aforementioned eclectic ramblings are a good or bad thing, relevant or not is of course dependent upon your own individual personal circumstances…but isn't it nice to know that this would be a better world if only we could *learn to share.*

Generosity and kindness happen to be of the noblest and most rewarding of human activities, and (cue a choir of angels with trumpets trumpeting) are a route to *becoming more.* Sitting Bull knew this …*remember him?*

Some would consider that those who act in contravention of the above could be construed as acting narrow-mindedly against the progression, elevation, evolution and overall growth of our species…but then again we are in universal terms not only seemingly arbitrary but also at an embryonic stage of capriciousness. Evolution quite naturally determines that each and every one of us will individually be at a different stage of our existential developmental progress – which will be evident in our individual, personal values.

… So perhaps we shouldn't expect to crawl before we can crawl.

In any case I'm wondering if you realise that *the rest of population don't actually don't have to live by the expectations you place upon them* – but then again…you neither have to live by theirs.

Quid pro quo.

Help! You're Self(s)

You should never become someone that you aren't…you should certainly never ever become someone that you don't like.

So, let us begin this section with a question of identity; *which version of you is the most important?*

- *The way you were,*
- *The way you are*

    or

- *The way you are going to be?*

You may be a tad confused right now, but think on it! For a start those versions of you are not one and the same.

I recently gazed upon a long forgotten 33 year old picture of the younger version of me; a newspaper cutting that came quite unexpectedly into my possession via my dead mother in what can only be described as a very strange coincidence . Funnily enough by way of a tie-in with an earlier tale in this text it features me and the School athletic team in our running uniform following the championship that I wrote of. *The point in relative terms to this is that I actually wrote that section of the book some months before the photograph surfaced.* Anyway, to the point. In many ways that person is a stranger to the current version of me. My abilities have changed; I am on an entirely different emotional level, have knowledge, experience, confidence and awareness's completely beyond my younger self's imagination and am on an entirely different cognitive and spiritual plane.

I have evolved.

Oh, and here's the other thing, I physically look completely different – this probably because *the person in that picture is not actually biologically me at all*…barely even one bit…and neither will be the future version of me be!

Wait…what?

Yes indeed. What you are about to read might just shock you;

Me, Myself and I

Your physical existence is comprised entirely of cells; literally trillions and trillions of them…in fact your composite cellular material consists of many times more cells than there are stars in the Milky Way!

Each individual cell is in itself a living being made up individually of over 50,000 different proteins and these are made of infinitesimal molecules. With no consciousness or will each cell has no singular purpose other than to comprise part of a greater whole; these miniscule building blocks form huge biological structures known as organs or body parts to carry out vital bodily functions, you know like a heart, a brain, lungs, skin, bones etc. In this way they literally gather resources and carry every physical function out.

You unquestionably need your cells as you can't physically exist without them, but as much as I hate to be the bearer of bad news…they don't actually need you!

Your cells can in fact survive without you for quite some time.

Okay, in keeping with the conundrum of all other quantum particle behaviour there is a further twist – microscopic quantum particles do not conform to the conventional laws of macroscopic objects. Paradoxically billions of your cells can be extracted from you and successfully transplanted into another person where they will happily live on. So you can actually physically expire and not physically exist anymore, but your transplanted cells would live on as part of someone else…so, part of what was you could become part of someone else and would still be alive as part of another biological amalgamation, whilst still being part of you …which at that point wouldn't actually exist at all.

Now, back to the old newspaper picture of me; the conventional image we hold of ourselves as a rigidly, defined static thing is wholly untenable because in reality all of your cells will die many times over in your lifetime…in fact 250 million of your cells have died since you began to read about your cells 120 seconds ago! Statistically 1-3 million of your cells die per second. This means in a 7 year period virtually all of your cells will have been totally replaced at least once…and every time your cell setup changes you are physically significantly different from before…because you are a new cellular version of you. If you are blessed enough to survive until a ripe old age you will have cycled through a million billion cells …so what you consider yourself at any point in time is really as much of a snapshot as a photograph.

Let's take this just a little further…your DNA makes each of your cells you, they form the you template based upon your genealogical hereditary evolution which goes back many thousands of years…but contrary to popular emotionally based opinion DNA does not remain constant or fixed, it is constantly mutating in reaction to your external environmental influences, merging with bacteria etc. Thus, the YOU template is always subtly tweaking and changing.

The biggest physical changes take place especially in the brain where the average neuron will have up to 1000 more mutations in its code than any other average bodily cell! A part of you is dying constantly. You are made of trillions of little things that are constantly changing, dying, regenerating;

The human body is in a perpetual and parallel state of destruction and construction!

So, all of this goes to explain why the version of me in the 33 year old photograph does not look like me…in that time I have completely regenerated not once, or even twice…but almost 5 times.

…Physically that person has not existed at all for 26 years.

Oh yes…contemplate that!

And as you may think about that I should explain further at this juncture that no matter what you think you are or are not ...you are so much more and so much less than that – as should now be becoming evident. If you change the way that you look at things, the things that you look at change, as does your "reality"; so let's indulge this just a little further.

Whilst we are discussing cells you now know that in relation to quantum mechanics, those cells that comprise you consist themselves of infinitesimal subatomic particles, so read on...

Now, at this stage it must be said that 99% of statistics are flawed, mostly because they are generally used out-with the context of accuracy. They can be malleable which is why on 55% of occasions I only use 72% of available percentages 14% of the time. However percentages aside did you know that statistically those cells of yours have a greater percentage of empty space than solid matter? *"Who cares...so what?"* you may say...well I care and here's what;

- *You, everyone else and everything else actually physically consists of more empty space than solid matter...every solid object that you will encounter does. The only reason that you don't reach out to touch your coffee table and find that your hand falls right through it (much like a ghostly spectre) or you cant walk straight through a brick wall is because everything is vibrating at the same rate that you are!*

Like a motor vehicle you are the subtotal of a collection of many parts. Oh, and another thing; the infinitesimal microscopic subatomic particles that you are made of do not actually conform to the laws that determine the behaviour of the macrocosmic collective. They can communicate with each other instantaneously over staggering distances, The concept that is wave/particle duality dictates that something can be one thing and another entirely different thing, and that the act of observation literally changes how they behave. Quite unlike macroscopic objects as described above they *can* pass through solid matter as if it were not there at all! So, how might the realisation that the tiny things that comprise you are behaving like this *right now change your perception of your reality* I wonder?

...Contemplate that.

Anyway, in any case we do so like to label things, including ourselves; when we do so it is classified as an *Identity statement*. People generalise because thinking about complex paradigms or concepts requires a lot of effort – it's hard! Remember, humans tend to follow the path of least resistance. So Identity statements are an easy, standardised form of classification that defines our collective, singular form. For example I can outline my own identity in so many different ways;

Grandson, Son, Husband, Father, Brother, Cousin, Friend, Neighbour, Writer, Hypnotherapist, NLP practitioner, Driver, Runner, Coffee drinker, Bass guitarist, Singer, Woodworker, Walker, Talker, Stickleback Stalker, Tree house builder, Contemplator, noodle eater... etc, etc.

I could go on and on.

Regardless, I am so much more than any of those identity statements...*does that make sense to you?* Listen out for the way others will label your or more importantly *their* identity in their every day communications – these definitions are often accompanied by belief statements. This can all prove very revealing indeed;

- *"I'm a smoker (identity) because it eases stress (Belief – It isn't/unreal reality)"*,
- *"I'm an alcoholic (identity) because it runs in my family (Belief –It isn't/unreal reality)"*,

- *I'm fat (identity) due to my underactive thyroid gland (Belief underpinning an excuse– unlikely/You don't know unless you have been tested)"*
- *I am a nurse! (identity/It is – real reality based upon employment)*

These are ways of defining oneself and clearly outline self imposed limits that are based upon identity.

So, okay, you may smoke, drink far too much alcohol, be overweight and currently be employed as a nurse…but that's not who you actually are, *you are so much more than you think you are*. Nicotine is toxic, poisonous and does not ease stress, alcoholism is not hereditary and although I never use statistics over 99% of overweight people have a perfectly normally functioning thyroid gland…so by way of a bonus here is my top secret cure to combat the "Obesity Disease";

- *The secret weight loss cure   any more than you need is greed Learn to put less calorific digestible objects in your mouth and move your body around a lot more – nice new healthy habits! I promise the weight will fall off easily and …you will be cured!*

So simple, yet millions contribute huge sums of cash for what amounts to a carefully marketed product based upon that very advice in what is a multi billion industry!

Oh, and by the by, isn't it interesting that historically in western society only the rich could afford to be fat and many of the poor were thin – yet nowadays many of the rich strive to be thin and the poor are fat? Being skinny is the current fashion and that is why the modern celebrity cult of great and good literally starve themselves. Ask yourself this; how would this trend be received in the age of our hunter gatherer ancestors?

Well, I promise that you wont get fat reading this book…it is printed on 100% fat free paper! Even better still if you are reading the ebook version...it is 101% good for the environment because it's not made of trees.

Contemplate that!

- *Just because these things are the way you have been, or are the way that you currently are...they needn't be the way you are going to be!*

A lump of clay is an amalgamation of universal subatomic particles, it is part of the Earth, it is then removed from the ground and shaped into the shape of a figure, and the figure is then called a statue by some or an ornament by others, it can then be called a piece of art, it is then bought and becomes a possession. In time it is passed on as either an heirloom or discarded as a piece of junk. So what then is it? An amalgamation of universal subatomic particles, a piece of Earth, a lump of clay, a figure, a statue or a piece of art, a possession, a heirloom, a piece of junk...or is it all, some, none of those things or not none of those things but not something else?

And now - the paradigm shift of self(s);

The differing portrayals of *your* own personal "*self*" actually amount to what is *a collection of quite unique personas*. What does this mean? Well essentially it means that you actually have no singular, consistent, constant fixed version of you that applies to all life situations or circumstances.

You are malleable and will have adopted many different sets of identities for a wide array of your life situations. How so? Well, the way that *you* portray yourself in each separate set of life's circumstances will *be* quite different to the way that you are or portray yourself in another. This is *good and* this is *healthy*. For example you will have a distinct persona at home with your partner, and this will be different from the one that you adopt in your relationships with your children, your own parents, siblings and friends. Further to this you will have a quite different persona that you will inhabit when you are at work with work colleagues, clients or casual acquaintances. Hardly surprising really, but research reveals that the brain is the responsible party - constructing distinct identities for significant human inferential roles.

Human relationships are extremely complex. Recent research carried out by eminent social scientists has revealed that the ideas of a core or permanent self are nothing more than illusory…a veritable fallacy. Yet in Western culture the fallacy of a singular, rigid core self is predominant, being central to many of our cultural institutions; the reality is that there is no fixed "*You*"…there are *many versions of "You"* dependent upon your environment and company.

So, back to my original question - *which version of you is the most important?*

The Mind(s)…

You are comprised of many parts and you should now know by now that you have a conscious mind and that you have an unconscious mind.

And by the by I am glad *you are both reading this*; thank you for allowing *me* to *speak to the other* through *you* so far…it will do *you* both *good*.

I have discussed the unconscious mind frequently throughout this book, and mentioned the term *subliminal* once or twice so let's explore this and what it all means. At this juncture you may also have previously have heard of the term *subconscious* mind. For the purpose of this text and my workings in this area I mostly use the terminology *Unconscious mind*. In essence they allude to the exact same thing. Personally I don't care what you or anyone else calls it - you could call it "ice cream and jelly" for all I care.

After all if it quacks, has webbed feet, lives in a puddle, waddles about on dry land and gets a kick out of eating bread then a duck is a duck.

- *Something is always what it is; it is never something else… unless of course it is neither both or more than that!*

Many scientists, professional health practitioners and any multitude of others either reject or knowingly occlude the very concept of the unconscious or subconscious mind…*they are either completely wrong or knowingly being sinister*. Be warned. I want to assure you in the strongest possible terms at this juncture that despite this there are those out there who actively seek to manipulate you and exploit others at this level for their own gain. Indeed, they may be denying the existence of the unconscious mind because in many cases they don't want you to accept it's existence and consequentially become forewarned and forearmed! Milton Erickson knew this; his vision and the application of his techniques was based purely on a strategic intent of benevolence. He knew the ramifications of the utilisation of his techniques for the reverse and opposite of this. Those actively acting in contravention of Milton Erickson's code of ethics will either manipulate the public themselves or readily employ those who know how to manipulate you on an unconscious level via all manner of language patterns, imagery, embedded commands and evocative anchoring techniques, etc.

They all know that peoples insecurities drive them to overcompensation and excess. Our good old friend Sigmund Freud did not operate on a strategic intent of benevolence. Quite the opposite. His intent was to create an atmosphere of reliance and need to enable for advantageous gain. He essentially considered people to be animals; a peculiar type of animal easily manipulated, none more so than when in large groups! By applying those principals' and with that mindset marketers come up with persistent and ever more creative ideas to sell products whilst getting rich in the process. They know and understand only too well that if you tap into the insecurities of an individual you can poke at their feelings of inadequacy and make them open to influence. This is the blueprint of modern day marketing; the cleverest marketing ploys hinge on finding the pain point of the consumer, making them feel even worse…then selling them a product that will make them feel better and thus being associated with making everything "alright!" Oh, and before I forgetfully forget have you noticed the similarity of this tactic with that of political parties, religions and elite groups of all ilk, etc?

Wow…now isn't that quite a case of serendipity!

Is there a solution? Well wouldn't it be better if we, the people were better able to develop an increased sense of self awareness to facilitate for a better understanding of the pandemic, corruptive tactics of the mass media. To know when they are probing on an unconscious level for our insecurities, weaknesses and vulnerabilities…and enable for a more appropriate mindset intent on personal protection from what purely amounts to subterfuge.

Oh yes, they *know the traits of the Unconscious mind,* and so dear reader …*it's* now time *you should* to.

Like consciousness, all of the facets of the mind are actually a nominalisation…that is it has no physical manifest and unlike a brain cannot be removed, put into a sports bag and carried around on a daily basis (well, there are some strange people around!) So, when I discuss the conscious and unconscious minds I am referring to a conceptual paradigm and not a literal aspect or part(s)…so, that being said let us continue;

I really want to help you to help *you* to *understand* the concept and role of the unconscious mind because *you can achieve almost anything through the* almost limitless *power of your unconscious mind*….you just need to *know how*. It can be directed if *you learn how*.

And when I have communicated with your conscious mind in this book I have done so like this; and when *I have communicated with your unconscious mind* I did and do so *like this*.

The influence of the unconscious mind can definitely maybe become problematic for the overall wellbeing of an individual if care is not taken. That is what this section is about because it does need to be understood and managed properly….crucially it needs *clear orders to follow* and does *operate in the realm of metaphor and symbology*.

Butterflies

When building my consultation room one hot spring I was becoming more aware…more aware… of me…my rural surroundings, the intricate songs of the birds from the deep woods, the rustling of the leaves in the gentle breeze, how intense the colours had become…in particular the flowers…and you can realise… it's odd how you learn to delete the things that surround us.

When you take the time to …notice…connect with nature…our Empress… you can…learn lessons from her creatures …which can be applied in our own lives. I noticed a beautiful butterfly land close to me on the wooden deck, this in spite of my presence as I sat there. Time slowed down as I studied its nuances and intricate details. And as I added meaningless meanings I contemplated the transformation that a butterfly goes through…from egg… to larva… to pupa…before it emerges in all of its glory.

And deep down I knew we were one.

I did… notice the experience… repeating many times…the butterfly reappearing time and time again as the days went by and the structure took shape…

At some point there was a sudden realisation that I had generalised and that it was not one and the same butterfly…each one was just another one of a particular species…alike but different. And I remembered myself…

In a way that was quite random I began to distort my experiences… as imagination can wonder…immersed….and as funny as it may sound for some reason I began to equate what was being experienced to the movie derived of William's Tempest - "Forbidden Planet" …and my own construction to that of the home of Dr Morbius…

…but then I realised that all of this is all, just all in the mind.

Chew on that, and then why not *contemplate this;*

You must understand and remember this before proceeding any further!

There is at this time only a reasonable conscious understanding of the conscious mind but very little conscious understanding of the unconscious mind. There are things that we know we know and things that we know that we don't know…but let's not forget the things that we don't know that we don't know now… no? Yet … the unconscious has a good unconscious understanding of the conscious mind, which in itself has little conscious understanding of this unconscious conscious understanding that the unconscious has on both an unconscious yet conscious level. And, I can consciously and unconsciously communicate with you on a conscious level and I can consciously and unconsciously communicate with you on an unconscious level, which I will, do and am. During this my unconscious will be communicating with my own conscious and yours will unconsciously be doing likewise and I will be noticing your unconscious communications to us both…so now you can understand that there is a constant communication loop between not only different parts that are us but also them all.

Have you got that?

Now the above may seem confusing, which it is - but in fairness it was meant to be …

I overloaded your conscious capacity, which in fairness is not difficult to do (no offence!) As a participant in the human living experience you are literally bombarded with millions of pieces of data, information and sensual input each and every second;

- The critical, analytical and reasoning conscious mind has an *extremely* limited capacity for any significant amount of absorption of the immeasurable experiential life events as they occur; in general terms it can only handle 7 plus or minus 2 pieces of information (7 + or – 2 = 9 or 5). This means that it filters out incredibly vast pieces of this information via a process of generalisation, distortion and deletion

…and this is where the unconscious mind steps in to ease the burden….to serve;

- The unconscious mind can multi-task and do a staggering volume of things at once – *running the body* whilst *sifting through up to TEN MILLION pieces of sensory information every second…*filtering out, protecting and passing on that which it thinks is important to conscious awareness.

There are some crucial factors that you need to understand about the unconscious mind, so sit back, plug in and switch on;

It stands to reason that the functioning biological and cognitive cybernetic system that constitutes an individual necessitates that both cognitive systems, the unconscious and conscious minds, must work in tandem…or the subsequent misalignment will create pervasive, enduring problems.

- *The unconscious mind habitually forms...and vigorously/stubbornly protects...habits in its literal quest to assist the conscious mind by removing the overburden of information or focussed cognitive function -and thus the overall cybernetic system (you).*

Don't believe me? Well do you remember the first time you attempted to drive a car...how overwhelmingly difficult was it? You perhaps thought *"Aaaaaagh I'll never ever learn this!"* You were actually at the stage of learning entitled *Conscious Incompetence*; that is, your conscious mind was blown away by the sheer volume of kinaesthetic motor (get it?) skills, auditory stimulation, cognitive decisions and visual information that it had been exposed to; by the way you went through a similar process when *learning to walk*, but then *you* won't *remember that!*

- *That which is repeated becomes that which is habitual...neural pathways are formed and established. For this reason we are literally creatures of habit.*

And now you jump into your car and speed around the place without even giving it much (*if any*) thought at all. I'll also bet that on many of your familiar journeys you won't even remember large chunks of your trip. This is the stage of learning known as *Unconscious Competence*...oh, and by the way it is also a state of hypnotic trance *(if there is such a thing)*.

You don't actually drive; your unconscious mind does it for you!

The true nature of your Unconscious Mind;

- *Be careful what you say....it is always listening.* You can't switch your ears off.

- It assimilates all input to a *literal* degree. This part of your mind operates on the premise that *it's all about you*, therefore it takes everything personally.

- Whatever *you* do don't *think about an orange banana with purple spots.* Stop! I told you not to *do that*...yet I know that *you* will just *have* instantaneously *formed a mental picture* of one! You see, it does not tend to process negatives; and always seeks exploration…to expand horizons.

- *Your unconscious mind* assumes the *smooth running of your body*; all of the things that the conscious mind have no awareness of. It controls oxygen levels and blood circulation - ensures the function of the vital organs, it is the catalyst for all growth and healing.

- It eases the burden placed upon the conscious mind by adopting habits – and then protects them for the (perceived) good of the system. It creates both the itch and the subsequent automatic reflex to scratch; it instigates hair growth, digestion, nail growth and skin cell replacement.

- It generates energy. As can be seen the unconscious has a perpetual commitment to being the auto pilot of the body on a moment to moment life time basis. It is the deep well of learning's, emotions, feelings, thoughts, sights, sounds, skills…and memories.

- It is the realm of the powerful imagination. All things must first be imagined for them to be subsequently actioned upon. With this in mind it is reasonable to recognise that it is impossible to do *anything* without approval from the unconscious mind; even a basic function like going to the toilet must be at least imagined for a nano-second!

- As the realm of memories. The unconscious creates associations that relate to stored memories and stores them. Thoughts, emotions, relationships and habits from a vanished time in our history can suddenly be instantly recalled with no conscious will whatsoever by simply hearing a song or smelling a fragrance. At that point in time you will be likely to feel the same emotions from that remembered long forgotten time because of the link that was formulated by the unconscious; this evidences the fact that the unconscious does not understand the concept of time.

Remember - *all time is now.*

Icebergs

A time ago a man with a clever mind called Freud thought about the minds – but knew without knowing he knew wrong. He likened the conscious mind to the tip of an iceberg…and the unconscious to the underlying larger, unseen body of ice…that lay deep beneath the surface. He decreed the unconscious mind to be a dark, repressed place without realising that it can be the reverse and opposite of that, and this and is much more still…

If…you think about it… in real terms that is a very poor analogy as everyone everywhere knows that an average iceberg consists of 10% visible tip and 90% unseen draught, does it not?

A better analogy or sense of perspective and context …if you like…can perhaps be attained from likening the conscious mind to that of a sailing yacht…cutting through the waves…utilising the wind, the tide and current…inherent environmental elements…steering to maintain a course and reach destinations yet unseen…and the unconscious mind the vast, resourceful, deep, life sustaining ocean upon which it navigates.

The unconscious mind has a level of influence that is incredible in its vast capacity – some theories actually asserting that it has the capacity to remember everything…*everything*…that the individual has ever experienced from conception to physical death…and perhaps beyond. So, every person's life is predominantly determined on an unconscious level; such is the pervading influence of its contribution to our very being – yet most people have absolutely no awareness of this. We are *not* consciously in control of what we do on a day to day basis….the unconscious mind is *the powerful* part of the mind…the part that is really in control!

But it is wide open to influence. Hypnosis *(whatever that is!)* bypasses the conscious mind and directly enables for change to be both instigated and supported through utilisation of the unconscious mind;

How In-trancing

A student told me that he thought that …hypnosis is… not …a real phenomenon …and thus that… it is… not… real. He further stated that people just played along with hypnotists to make …it… look… real. Of course I told him that in that case he was right and that …hypnosis was …not…a real phenomenon. As I said this I nodded slowly and funnily enough he did too. I further explained that despite his correct assertion that… hypnosis was …not …real…many people enjoyed pretending to…go into trance…and that pretending to …go into a deep trance…allowed some people to …find new old learning's … deeper down inside…now, then, whenever or wherever…

I told him "If you forget to remember that thing that you want to remember to forget then you will have forgotten in a forgetful way to forget the thing that you wanted to forget and it's forgotten…do …you know what I mean?" And he didn't which was as it should be. You see some people find …going into a trance state… when …the brain downshifts into the Alpha and Theta state… right down…deep inside…a… very comforting and relaxing state to go into…which is good. I explained that when …in a moment…this is now happening …that …a person's… heart rate drops… breathing changes… and that… blood pressure eases. Indeed …deep progressive relaxation spreads through the muscles …a nice warm sensation…and… the feeling is comfortable and invigorating…as they forget their surroundings…in trance.

I couldn't help but notice that he had slipped away during all of this ...so I just spoke to his unconscious for awhile instead ...until...he returned...to... a fully alert state.

The unconscious does not reason, does not question or is not critical...it merely serves; in fact it is the most subservient of companions. Importantly;

The unconscious has tremendous, virtually limitless capacity for benevolence; however it also is frequently pivotal in maintaining negative, even destructive behaviours in people. All meaningful change occurs on an unconscious level...thus *whenever you are talking to someone else you are not just talking to what you or they think they are and what they actually are – you are actually talking to what they were and what they will be.*

- *When interacting with other humans I am acutely aware that I am interacting with the embryo, the child, the teenager, the adult, the elderly...the life force, the soul. You may laugh, but I am operating on that level of awareness whether you laugh...or not.*

You are wide open to literal influence; you need to be careful about the audible and internal dialogue in which you partake...the thoughts that you think. You should be careful of being around perpetually negative people...negativity is particularly invasive. You literally get what you focus on. Care must also be taken from external influence in this modern age of information. Nobody seems to *be interested in* that which is *subtle* anymore, the *nuances*. We are constantly bombarded by "noise" - advertising and communication from those with agenda driven strategies. For example lets take Kellyanne Conway, one of president Donald Trumps aides who laughably (I actually did laugh out loud!) asserted on live television that we'd got it all wrong, stating that his proven falsehoods (*aka Lies*) about the size of the crowd in attendance at his inauguration are actually "Alternative facts!" Wow, now that's what I call one hell of a reframe!

- *A classic ploy. They know that if you are right and they are wrong that if they tell you that you are wrong and not right again, and again, and again, and again that you will begin to doubt that you are right and will begin to accept that which is wrong is right...which is wrong and not right, right?*

So steps must be taken to protect ourselves from this type of subversion. We have already discussed how to increase control over our mind and its incessant activity; you now need to learn to build a fortress around it for defence against external manipulation.

Empowering verbal affirmations (or prayers if you prefer) and visualisations that are made on a constant basis will undoubtedly have a significant and beneficial impact upon the self. On an Unconscious level all things are being perpetually monitored, and be mindful that any imagined protective barrier is on this level...*real*;

Powerful White Aura Exercise

Control your breathing as outlined previously.

Imagine that you are surrounded by a powerful white aura of love; it wraps you in safety and comfort. It is invisible to the naked eye...only you can see it...but it is harder than the hardest known material to mankind. Picture seeing yourself surrounded by it...lift your hand and see the glow of this powerful aura of protection. Now make it stronger...then stronger still.

Negativity and bad intentions cannot breach it. Any negativity that you feel within is immediately dispelled from its safety and disperses into the atmosphere. As you breathe each exhalation fills the powerful white aura with rainbow coloured positivity...as you inhale this you feel calm, confident, relaxed...

Wear the powerful white aura everyday, apply it anywhere; in the car as you travel to work, sitting in your office…in the shower! Notice how this actually protects you and how it enhances your life.

Notice how others behave in your presence…on an unconscious level they will detect it.

This works and you should construct your own regularly because the unconscious does not know the difference between what is real or imagined. If *you imagine it*, then *it is real!* This is how *positive self affirmations, inner dialogue and prayer work.* The unconscious is the realm of the imagination!

- *Imagination allows us to envisage a future that we have yet to create!*

The unconscious mind is the powerful part of the mind – *imagination can trump knowledge.*

Your unconscious follows the path of least resistance – we are creatures of neurological and thus behavioural habit; but this can be detrimental. If *you* take the time to *notice* it is easy to uncover *the habits of others* by simply observing their patterns.

The unconscious mind is a willing servant with the sole purpose of facilitating the overall well being of the individual; but to do so it needs clear instruction and guidance. Clear goals, direction and control are needed; much like a chariot which is drawn by its team of stallions. This can be achieved through simple, verbal affirmations of intended goals and outcomes and clear and positive thoughts and self talk in the pursuit of such. Taking the time to thank your unconscious will never go unappreciated… do you *do so?*

The unconscious represses bad memories as well as organises them. The unconscious will repress bad memories and traumas in a protective capacity to ease the conscious minds exposure to unpleasantness. This may be initially beneficial in the immediate aftermath of such an event; however it may also be the catalyst for elongated unresolved problems based upon these unresolved, unacknowledged connected emotions. This can lead to long term symptoms of fear, guilt, hurt, anger and sadness. Problems that are buried deep within, which are effectively still "alive" will tend to dig their way out when least expected to the detriment of the persons well being. Sooner or later there is a need to acknowledge and deal with these events.

- *To do so may involve a power struggle with the unconscious…which as the most powerful part of the mind will always over power will power (which is conscious activity) and win unless manipulated in the appropriate manner.*

Once established through repetition it adopts and protects bad habits. The unconscious knows that the conscious mind can only realistically concentrate on one task at a time – as far as it is concerned *it is serving you* by taking on as many tasks as possible. It will take on these tasks in an attempt to unburden the conscious mind and subsequently form habits.

Remember it does not know the difference between good habits and bad habits, a habit is a habit regardless. Therefore it can unwittingly embed and guard phobias, anxiety and fear responses. It will guard drug addiction, alcoholism, obesity and so much more. This can lead to conflict…the conscious mind understanding that a destructive habit or behaviour needs to be addressed – but the unconscious still protecting that which it established as habit in an ongoing loop, it is a power struggle…and *the unconscious mind is much stronger than the conscious!*

It has a blueprint for perfect health…but this can become skewed. The hypochondriac is able to persuade themselves on an unconscious level that they are in fact suffering from physical sickness and limitations – the unconscious will often compromise on its blueprint and accept such limitations which will become manifest. Fortunately this works equally in reverse…this is why *placebo's are so effective.*

This aside, the unconscious is the heart of the innate survivalist;

The instinct to live

A troubled young lady said "I hate myself, self harm and am going to kill myself by jumping off a tall bridge" – I shouted "You're an idiot and you're very, very stupid! If you follow my perfect method on how to hurt and kill yourself properly you won't have to jump from a stupid tall bridge"…an effective pattern interrupt that admittedly took her somewhat by surprise judging by the shocked silence at the other end of the line. Her psychiatrist hadn't talked like that.

When she came along I said "Do you really want to hurt and kill yourself?" to which she replied in the affirmative. I said "Well, prove it then! Now is the time for you to hurt and kill yourself properly with my perfect method, there is no need to cut your self – and a high bridge is entirely surplus to requirements." I told her "Do as I tell you when I tell you. Sit still, say goodbye, close your mouth tightly and keep it closed, pinch your nose hard and it'll be all over soon enough …now…breathe …no more…in a few minutes you will be dead"

Within more than less than a minute she gave in, gasping frantically for life…gasping for the sustaining air that she had denied wanting to breathe any more…

After a while she silently looked into my eyes and said "I don't want to self harm or kill myself anymore." And I said "That's right, you don't!"

Of course, I knew that all along. Her unconscious mind had initially told me that in the beginning…and had just provided further proof…

Why not contemplate all of this and *understand how* even the most basic understanding of *your unconscious mind can* be harnessed to *improve your life.*

So, be that as it may, may it as that be…

Consciousness

You now know that physiological cues can be considered as revealing but it is very difficult to know what exactly is really happening with another persons head...after all we cannot read another persons mind.

Sometimes you have to ask...

The human race has proudly produced some magnificent minds, and you actually have one that is also capable of magnificence. You can expand it, develop it, free it...even be out of it (using your preferred chemical method or extreme emotional state); but what actually is it? Attempting to clarify what a mind actually is can be very hard. You cannot locate it, pin it down or during an autopsy remove it from a dead body...yet you cannot live without it.

Such is its significance it is fair to assert that the mind is the very essence of your consciousness...and arguably what is often termed in popular culture and religion as *your spirit...or soul* .

It is you, and so much more!

Please read on;

Neuroscientists, psychiatrists and sociologists had traditionally concluded that the mind was a direct result of brain activity – yet modern studies notably led by Dan Siegel, a professor of psychiatry at UCLA School of medicine reveal a somewhat different hypothesis that sees a shift further away from this theory. It reveals increasing evidence that the workings of the mind may be much less solely a direct result of this neurological brain activity...that, despite the brain playing a vital role, the mind is not actually constrained within our brain, our skulls...or *our body!*

- *The pioneering assertion now is that, based upon increasing evidence the mind extends well beyond the physical being.*

Moreover all of your subjective experiences that define your existence may well be interconnected and intertwined with your mind; your feelings, thoughts, memories, interactions, relationships, sounds, smells, tastes, images…*everything*. Remember, everything that we experience is in real terms merely the brains neurological interpretation of an electrical stimulus provided by our senses.

This new understanding brings the theory of consciousness closer into line with the shocking theory promulgated by one of Einstein's primary protégés, David Bohm and the esteemed quantum physicist Karl Pribram that *we are actually living in what is in effect nothing more than a hallucinatory, holographic universe.*

If this is true this would mean that the mind, as a self utilised level of brain activity, an ecological way of being, is not solely restricted or isolated to just being you – it is part of a relational, collective consciousness. If this is the case then you, I and every other one of us are literally us; and …*all one*.

If true then we all are one in what is a collective unconscious consciousness.

At this point you may ask what does this mean. What are the implications of this?

Well, what are you asking me for? I never listened in school, *remember?* I just thought *you* would like to *contemplate that just like me!*

And if you think that this amounts to no more than crazy talk then that's your prerogative, just don't shoot the messenger. To counter this I would however remind you that all of this has come from some of the worlds most expansive, eminent and greatest of minds, those who are in *Mens Sana*;

… So keep yours open!!

So, how can the fact that all experience equates to nothing more than a neurological interpretation of an electrical stimulus assist us in our day to day lives? Well, it can be directly used to reduce physical and emotional pain;

Pain Control Technique

As previously taught begin to control your breathing, regulate it…breathe in for 4 seconds …and out for 5 seconds…and continue to do so. This is your cadence. Now, this may sound strange but that's okay, really consider this question;

What colour is your pain?

Notice that you can indeed define the colour of your pain. There is no wrong answer, what's right for you is right for you…and is. Everything is subjective. Go with your instinct.

Now for the next phase… as you continue with your breathing…in…and out…on those 5 second exhalations …you are going to focus on the wall facing you; you are going to paint it with your pain. Imagine …breathing out all of that coloured pain onto the wall…like paint. Keep going until in your minds eye…the wall is completely covered in that colour. Continue to do so as you give the wall another coat of that pain paint. Once you have finished why not give it another coat of pain paint.

This may take some time but once you have finished notice …how much better you feel!

Try it. Use it and practice it when you need relief. *It works* and by now you can imagine probably constructing some form of understanding why.

And now, the end of this book and our time together is near. It has been a blast however I have one final hypothetical question for you;

What would life be without hypothetical questions?

And so to finish up a simple reframe;

I have a car, nothing special, expensive or elaborate. After all I am a mere, humble and simple person. That aside I am rich, but only rich in so much as my riches consist of the type of currencies that are often overlooked and therefore unseen by many in the madness of this modern society. I'm lucky. Feeling the sun warm my skin and just noticing the uniqueness of a blade of grass, or even wrapping up against a cold night and admiring the stars in the night sky totally floats my boat and deposits large quantities of awe into my internal bank account! That apart, my monetary resources are admittedly finite. So my car is just a cheap second hand family car much like many thousands of others.

But did you know that my car runs on invisible planetary atmosphere?

Well, it does and so does yours.

Now, apologies for bursting your bubble but in-car entertainment, colour, fancy headlights, alloy wheels or a prestigious marque are not what matters. To those in the know tyres are considered the single most important part of a motor vehicle…yet essential and important as they undoubtedly are tyres are useless without air. So air fills the tyre and the tyre is in touch with the road surface …and we have a successful way of both rolling along and keeping a grip. *Thus air is the most important component of any car...be it a Ferrari, Lamborghini, Porsche...or a cheap second hand family car like mine.*

As sentient beings we are filled with invisible emotions, yet often we lack even the barest understanding of how we can not only be in touch with them ...but also roll along with them, keep a grip and manage them properly. Do *you see the connection?*

Contemplate that and this;

The Surfer

A man came to see me about his panic attacks...they were causing him all sorts of problems in his life. He said "I get this feeling and then they just wash over like waves me when I least expect them"

That was an interesting analogy, and sure enough it turned out that he was a surfer, so I told him "Nobody can ever completely stop waves of panic attacks, but the secret of managing of them lies not in stopping them or allowing them to crash into you ...but in successfully riding them." He understood that frame of reference.

I then said "What colour is the feeling you get before those waves of panic? And which way does that feeling spin?" which caused him to stop, and then go inside for a search to find out.

After that all I had to do was have him change the colour and spin the feeling backwards. In trance he learned to stop looking at what wasn't there and become adept at playing Pooh sticks...

Following our time together he learned how to ride the waves and assume control of his feelings...then it was all water under the bridge!

And on that note I'm sad to say that, for now our time together has come to an end; that is this book has now arrived at its furthermost extremity. As I now gaze back at what has been promulgated I catch myself wondering where it has all come from…before remembering that *I never actually wrote it; my unconscious mind did!*

I any case thanks for accompanying me, let's do it again some time.

So to conclude proceedings I'd like to leave you with just one final short story for your contemplation.

The Locust on the fence

In ancient China somewhere between the fourth and sixth centuries BCE there lived a hermit, a wise man of renowned renown. His name was Boddha. Now I must tell you that Boddha (not to be confused with Buddha, who was practicing at the same time and slightly more expensive to consult) lived a life of solitude in a mountain retreat far beyond the great forest and the great lake. Despite this his wisdom was oft sought by seekers of wisdom and the true path.

A young farmer lived beside his burgeoning crop with his fiancé in a relatively small yet comfortable cabin that he had built for him and his beautiful young bride to be. One day whilst tending his beloved crop he noticed a locust sitting on his fence and wondered what this omen meant. That night there was a terrible storm. Fearing for his crop he raced outside to save as much of it as he could. As he went outside one of his windows blew open and the wind knocked a lit candle over; his cabin burnt to the ground, including his life savings which were hidden under the floor and his crop was destroyed. Disgusted, his fiancé left him for another wealthier farmer.

Inconsolable the tortured farmer kept asking himself and anyone who would listen over and over *"Why, why, why has this happened to me?"* The village elder **eventually** said *"travel through the dense forest, over the great lake and up the mountain to visit Boddha, he will gift you with the wisdom and perspective you require!"*

The farmer did just that. After a long and arduous journey he came to Boddha, who was sitting serenely in meditation in the lotus position beside a waterfall in a small clearing overlooking a valley as wind chimes gently chimed in a soft breeze. *"And what I wonder do you seek?"* he asked the farmer without breaking state or opening his eyes. The farmer relayed his sad tale from the beginning, starting with the sighting of the locust on the fence to the loss of his material wealth and betrothed. An inanimate Boddha did not break state, he simply listened and simply was. After some time Boddha said *"I must contemplate all of this and then I will give you wisdom. Please come back tomorrow."*

The farmer did so and asked **yet again** for wisdom. Again Boddha (still in deep meditation and the lotus position) said *"I need to consult Om, the seed of the universe, the creator, the divine cosmos further. Come back tomorrow and I will give you wisdom."*

This **pattern** continued for two weeks. On the fifteenth day, the farmer once more sought audience and once more asked Boddha for wisdom. At last he finally opened his eyes, gazed with compassion and empathy upon the poor farmer and stated *"I have what you seek; wisdom and perspective. Come closer"* – the farmer eagerly did so and Boddha said *"Come closer still"*…then gently whispered into the **farmer's** ear;

"Dude, sometimes shit just happens. Regardless of why what has happened, if you cannot change the situation… you are challenged to change yourself!"

~The End ~

ABOUT THE AUTHOR

John Glyn Hughes is a Master NLP Practioner and Coach, Hypnotherapist and Trainer. Working from his small, intimate practice based in Helensburgh, Argyll, Scotland he is the founder of align nlp & hypnotherapy. His hobbies include writing, playing bass guitar and singing in a band, furniture design and build, jogging, walking and enjoying mother nature.

The author is available for one to one & group nlp & hypnotherapy sessions and is always particularly keen to receive feedback on any of the content of this title and can be contacted at;

alignnlp@mail.com

For further information on John Glyn Hughes or align nlp & hypnotherapy please visit;

www.alignnlp.co.uk

Printed in Great Britain
by Amazon